mmits
or all

D1313232

Copyright of the original French edition © 1991 by
Editions Franck Mercier, Annecy
Copyright in the English translation © 1992 by Cordee, Leicester

ISBN 1 871890 26 8

British Library Cataloguing in Publication Data
A catalogue record for this book is available from the British Library

Both the author and publisher have made great efforts in the compilation
of this guide book. However, as it is the work of human beings and as
mountains can change, errors and discrepancies cannot be ruled out.
Therefore, no guarantee can be given for the accuracy of every piece of
information. No legal liability is accepted for any accidents or damages
sustained for whatever reason.

All trade enquiries to:
Cordee, 3a De Montfort Street, Leicester LE1 7HD
All trade enquiries in France to:
Editions Franck Mercier, BP 404, 74013 Annecy

This guide book is available from all specialist equipment shops and
major booksellers. It can, along with all the maps mentioned in the text
be obtained direct from the publishers. Please write for a copy of our
comprehensive stocklist of outdoor recreation and travel books/maps.

CORDEE
3a De Montfort Street, Leicester, Great Britain, LE1 7HD

Summits
for all

100 EASY MOUNTAINS
FOR WALKERS

EDOUARD PREVOST

Edited from an original translation by Jill Neate

Cordee – Leicester, Great Britain

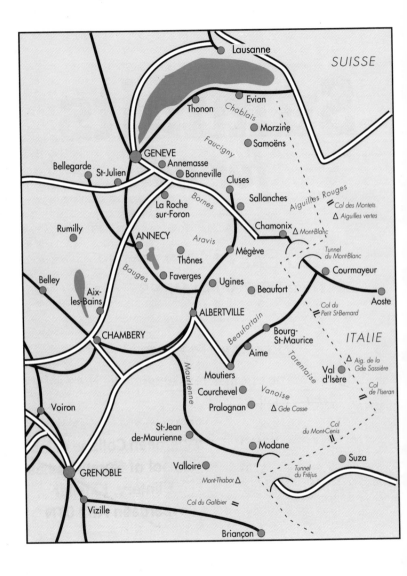

preface

The French alpine regions of Savoie and Haute-Savoie located south of Lake Geneva contain scores of beautiful mountains of modest height and difficulty, but allowing wonderful views of the nearby giants of the Alps. Often tucked away in secluded valleys hidden from the bustle of the main tourist centres, the beauty of these mountains cannot be overstated. The well positioned refuges and gites d'étape high in the mountains, offering meals, drinks and accommodation, add a leisurely quality to the day.

The value of this selected guide is its scope. Edouard Prevost has selected 100 routes in the mountains of Chablais-Faucigny, Aiguilles Rouges de Chamonix, Bornes, Aravis, Bauges, Beaufortain and Vanoise-Tarentaise. He gives a body of information that will allow a hill walker to move easily from one mountain group to another during a holiday to sample the little known delights of this part of the French Alps.

The routes on these mountains are not a serious challenge; they are usually the most logical line to the top and, for an experienced British hill walking party, they present no great difficulties under normal summer conditions. Fitness and acclimatization may be necessary for some. All you will then need are settled weather and a suitably early start to ensure success.

THE ROUTES

Most of the routes in this guidebook are day trips, much like any day on the British mountains. A few of the longer routes have been described as two day outings using alpine (CAF) huts or private refuges as overnight accommodation. Even these longer routes can be undertaken in one day by a fit party.

The variety of the routes is considerable, ranging from those over flower covered meadows and wooded terrain involving only modest ascent, to strenuous climbs traversing rugged slopes, with scrambling up steep ground, along exposed ridges, with steep snowslopes and easy glaciers to negotiate. The approach paths are mostly well defined and waymarked. Any prolonged climb up will be helped by well constructed zig-zags.

Early in the season (mid June) large areas of snow (nevés) can cover sections of the paths above 2000m and in the morning are often hard and icy. As summer progresses these melt away, but can always be present on some north facing slopes, in gullies and stream beds. They present the hill walker with a situation demanding care and an ice axe.

The times given are those required for a small party (not over loaded) moving at an average pace under normal summer conditions and in good weather.

Difficulty

The routes are fully described and are classified simply according to difficulty:

Grade 1
Routes presenting no difficulties and suitable for beginners of all ages.

Grade 2
Routes involving some difficulties – rock scrambling and snow slopes, but not technical and well within the ability of British hill walkers who have been forewarned.

Grade 3
Routes involving a fairly low level of alpine climbing technical difficulty, but sometimes necessitating the use of a rope, ice axe or crampons. Scrambling over rock faces, exposed ridges, snow slopes, loose scree and easy glaciers. This grade is therefore only for the hill walker of all round experience who is confident on such terrain in the British mountains.

Certain routes in this guide suggest the carrying of such equipment as a rope, ice axe and crampons. It is strongly recommended that you have such equipment with you, and know how and when to use it for the routes in question.

LOCATION OF THE ROUTES

This guide gives sufficient information so that apart from the appropriate large scale detailed map (I.G.N. or Didier & Richard) mentioned in the text, no further references are necessary for the mountain. To find the starting point for each route, use should be made of a local road map (Michelin sheet 89 or I.G.N. sheet 112 red series) reference is made to the well known towns of the area, and clear directions are given from these.

EQUIPMENT

Experienced mountain walkers need no lessons on equipping themselves appropriately. What applies to the British mountains is the same for the routes here but take extra care against the ravages of the sun by using good sun glasses/goggles and sun cream. Inexperienced people should read 'Safety on Mountains' published by the British Mountaineering Council.

DANGERS

There is an element of risk in alpine walking which even the best prepared cannot guard against. There may be little likelihood of danger, but occasionally events occur in which the situation is serious, and you will be called upon to act. If there is a refuge or chalet in the area help can be summoned by telephone to the mountain rescue service or police. Know the international distress call **Six times in a minute a visible or audible signal.** Reply, that the message has been understood, **Three times per minute.** To signal to an helicopter with one arm means, "No do not land, we do not require anything." Both arms above the head means "Help! Please land".

WEATHER

Being aware of the weather patterns and conversant with the signs which occur before a change are important elements in mountain safety. Such knowledge for an area like this is beyond the scope of this guide. Bad weather and storms are a significant danger and you should not continue on your route if the weather is threatening.

Detailed weather forecasts are displayed each morning at tourist information offices throughout the region. Pre-recorded weather forecasts are available by telephoning the 'Meteo'. (50) 53.03.40.

1. CHABLAIS-FAUCIGNY

1. Dent d'Oche
2. Cornettes de Bise
3. Pointe de Grange
4. Pointe de Chesery
5. Les Hauts Forts
6. Les Dents Blanches
7. Roc de Tavaneuse
8. Pointe de Nantaux
9. Mont Billiat
10. Pointe d'Ireuse
11. Roc d'Enfer
12. Le Mole
13. Tête du Colloney
14. Aiguille de Varan
15. Pointe d'Ayère
16. Mont Buet

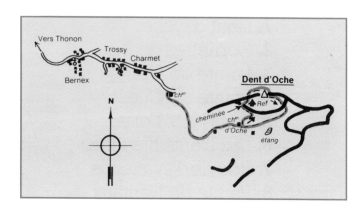

01 Dent d'Oche

- height: 2,222 m
- starting point: Bernex, 15 km east of Thonon
- route: from the south
- grade: I
- climbing time: 3 hours
- views: very beautiful
- type of ground: woodland, grass, stones, scree, rocks
- IGN map: 3528 ET – 1:25 000 Didier Richard No 3 – 1:50 000
- d'Oche Hut (CAF)
  hut warden Tel: 50 73 62 45

Access: At Thonon take the N5 in the direction of Evian and leave it shortly after at Vongy, where one turns right immediately after the bridge over the River Dranse. Carry on through Publier and Saint-Paul as far as Bernex. Continue beyond Bernex for about 3 km, taking care to follow the signs to the CAF d'Oche Hut (first road on the right after the hamlet of Trossy). Leave vehicles at a car park by a bar-restaurant chalet (alt. 1,050 m).

Ascent: Behind the chalet, take a good path which rises through the forest to the Chalets d'Oche (alt. 1,650 m), sited on a flat area at the bottom of a large valley. To the left the Dent d'Oche dominates the chalets with its imposing mass. Ignore the tracks which climb the valley to the right of the cliff face and start up to the left in the direction of the lower slopes of the Dent d'Oche. The well marked path goes up a steep, stony slope (way-marked in yellow) and arrives at the face at the foot of a steep couloir-chimney which is climbed with the aid of cables and iron railings. At the top of the chimney, emerge on to a rocky platform by the d'Oche Hut (alt. 2,150 m). This construction seems alien in this rocky neighbourhood. Continue behind the hut up the exposed path, cross an easy rock section and reach the summit.

Descent: Descend by the same route. It is equally possible to continue along the summit ridge and descend the previously described valley by a higher route, down to the Chalets d'Oche.

Route notes

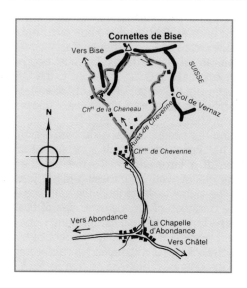

02 Cornettes de Bise

- height: 2,432 m
- starting point: La Chapelle d'Abondance, 33 km east of Thonon
- route: from the west
- grade: I
- climbing time: 4 hours
- views: very beautiful
- type of ground: grass, stones, scree
- IGN map: 3528 ET – 1:25 000   Didier Richard No 3 – 1:50 000
- Bise Hut (CAF)
  hut warden   Tel: 50 73 11 73

Access: At Thonon, take the N202 which goes through the gorge of the River Dranse for 11 km, then turn left and follow the D22 as far as La Chapelle d'Abondance. In the village, take the little road on the left signposted to Chevenne and follow it to the end of the asphalted section by a bridge just before the Chalets de Chevenne. Leave vehicles here (alt. 1,216 m).
N.B.: Reach the Bise Hut after passing the Chalet de Cheneau, by descending north-westwards (30 min) or by car via Vacheresse (D222).

Ascent: Just before the bridge, take the good tracks on the right which follow the Chevenne stream (way-marked in red and white). After about ten minutes, leave these tracks, which lead to the Col de Vernaz, and take a path on the left which rises through a small wood (signposted to Les Cornettes via the Pas de la Bosse). Reach the Chalet de la Cheneau situated on a flat area. On the right one can make out the important rocky mass headed by the summit of the Cornettes de Bise. Continue past the chalet and, via a grassy slope, reach a second flat area just before the next slope. Here, by the flat area (ruined chalet), leave the path and aim well to the right towards the cliff face, so as to rejoin at its foot the path coming up from the Chalets de Bise (to the north-west). On good tracks ascend a large, stony and very steep couloir which splits the face. Higher up follow from left to right a ridge which includes several exposed sections and emerges on to the crest. Then turn left to reach the frontier summit (France-Switzerland).

Descent: Descend by the same route. However, it is possible to return by the following route: descend from the summit and, leaving the ascent couloir on the right, turn south-eastwards towards a ruined hut, sited on the frontier crest and visible from the Cornettes de Bise. Pass below this hut and work to the right, descending into a valley which takes you back to the starting point.

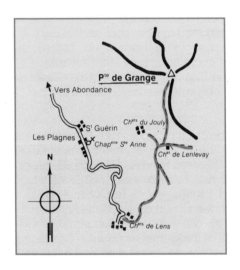

03 Pointe de Grange

- height: 2,433 m
- starting point: Abondance, 27 km south-east of Thonon-les-Bains
- route: from the south
- grade: I
- climbing time: 2 hours 30
- views: very beautiful
- type of ground: woodland, grass
- IGN map: 3528 ET – 1:25 000   Didier Richard No 3 – 1:50 000

Access: At Thonon-les-Bains, take the N202 which follows the gorge of the River Dranse. After 11 km turn off left and follow the D22 to Abondance. In the village cross the river to the right, ascend as far as the last of the houses and, at a fork, take a small road on the left signposted to Charmy-l'Adroit (V3) and go along the base of the Grange mountain. Follow the road beyond Les Plagnes, where the asphalted surface ends. After a long series of zig-zags up a fairly steep slope, one arrives at the Chalets de Lens (alt. 1,588 m). Leave vehicles by the first chalets, slightly set back from the road on the left.

Ascent: From these first chalets, take a good track which leads northwards and climbs a short wooded section. On leaving the wood, one arrives at a very open, flat crest from where the Pointe de Grange is visible to the north. Ignore a path on the left which leads to the Chalets du Jouly and continue as far as the Chalet de Lenlevay (alt. 1,740 m), quite nearby. Then leave the large track, which leads eastwards, and look for a path above the hut, not easy to find and rather poorly marked on a slope scattered with trees and brushwood. Emerge on to a long grassy crest and follow it northwards. Ascend some steep sections to the summit which forms the end of the ridge.

Descent: Descend by the same route.

Route notes

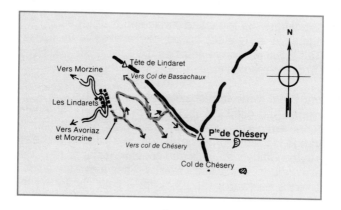

04   Pointe de Chesery

- height: 2,251 m
- starting point: Morzine
- route: from the north-west
- grade: I
- climbing time: 2 hours
- views: very beautiful
- type of ground: grass
- IGN map: 3528 ET – 1:25 000   Didier Richard No 3 – 1:50 000

Access: From Morzine via Montriond and Lac de Montriond (D228) to Les Lindarets. Go right through the small village and leave vehicles on a big flat area below the road, on the left, level with the starting point of a ski lift (alt. 1,500 m).

Ascent: Follow briefly the dirt track which crosses the flat part, up to a signpost indicating two routes to the Col de Chésery. Take the left hand one which leads also to the Col de Bassachaux. The very well-marked and not very steep path rises firstly northwards, then turns south-east across a slope scattered with conifers. Reach a flat, open area (alt. 1,800 m) where there is a signpost and high tension pylon. Ignore the paths which lead left to the Col de Bassachaux and right to the Col de Chésery. Go straight up the slope (no tracks) in the direction of the long crest to the east and join it at a point where it is practically horizontal. Turn right and follow the crest which gradually rears up and leads easily to the summit.

Descent: Descend by the same route.

Route notes

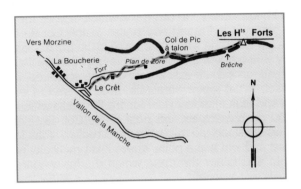

05　Les Hauts Forts

- height: 2,464 m
- starting point: Morzine
- route: from the west
- grade: I
- climbing time: 4 hours
- views: very beautiful
- type of ground: woodland, grass
- IGN map: 3528 ET – 1:25 000　　Didier Richard No 3 – 1:50 000

Access: South of Morzine, take the small road along the little La Manche valley and follow it for about 2.5 km as far as a signpost, on the left hand side of the road, to the locality of Le Crêt. Here, turn left down a track suitable for motors which leads to the houses and leave vehicles on a small car park on the right just beyond a bridge (alt. 1,100 m).

Ascent: Opposite the car park, climb up a meadow (no path to start with) on the right of a stream and make for a wood. Climb the steep, wooded slope following a well marked path. Pass in front of an abandoned chalet and a little higher up, reach the base of a vast sloping pasture and ascend it. Cross the Plan de Zore (alt. 1,800 m) and continue towards the top of the slope as far as the Col du Pic à Talon (alt. 2,043 m). Turn right (east) and follow the crest of the hill, broad and almost flat, to a point where it narrows. Descend carefully into the gap and ascend the other side (tricky section), then continue on the crest, now broad again, to the summit.

Descent: Descend by the same route.

Route notes

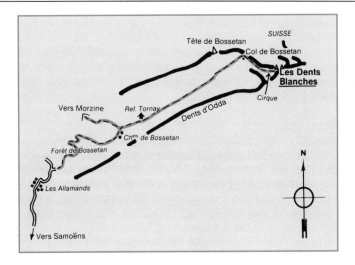

06   Les Dents Blanches

- height: 2,696 m
- starting point: Samoëns, 21 km east of Cluses
- route: from the south-west
- grade: II
- climbing time: 1st day: 2 hours; 2nd day: 3 hours 30 minutes
- views: very beautiful
- type of ground: woodland, stones, scree
- equipment necessary: rope, ice axe
- IGN map: 3530 ET – 1:25 000   Didier Richard No 3 – 1:50 000
- Tornay Hut (community property) hut warden   Tel: 50 90 10 94

Access: At Cluses, take the N202 to Taninges and then the N507 as far as Samoëns. At the exit from the village, in the direction of Sixt, go left on a small road which leads to the hamlet of Les Allamands (alt. 1,050 m). Continue beyond the houses for some 500 metres on a track suitable for motors. Take a second track on the right (signposted to Bossetan) and leave vehicles immediately afterwards on a lay-by (alt. 1,100 m).

Ascent:
First day: Climb up through a dense forest on the good track which leads to the Chalets de Bossetan (alt. 1,602 m), situated above the last fir trees, at the bottom of the small valley of the Col de Bossetan. Ascend the valley a little way, keeping well to the left, to reach the small Tornay Hut (alt. 1,763 m), property of the CAF and wardened in the summer.
Second day: Continue up the small valley which is bordered on the right by the long rocky crest of the Dents d'Odda. Go to the very end of the valley, keeping always to the left, to reach the Col de Bossetan (alt. 2,290 m), situated on the frontier crest between France and Switzerland and dominated on the extreme right by Les Dents Blanches. Turn right and follow the crest on the Swiss side and, through a broad gap, enter a small cirque. Ascend a broad couloir on the left, often covered by hard snow. If this slope is snowed up, do not hesitate to rope up and use ice axes. Emerge on to the first summit, then turn eastwards on a short, sharp ridge to reach the second summit.

Descent: Descend by the same route.

Route notes

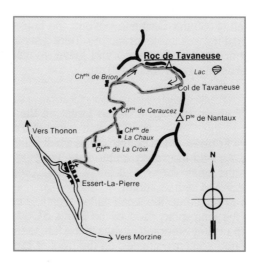

07   Roc de Tavaneuse

- height: 2,156 m
- starting point: Morzine
- route: from the south-west
- grade: I
- climbing time: 4 hours
- views: very beautiful
- type of ground: woodland, grass
- IGN map: 3530 ET – 1:25 000   Didier Richard No 3 – 1:50 000

Access: At Morzine, take the Thonon road and follow it for about 3 km as far as the bridge at Plagnettes. Continue for a few hundred metres (still towards Thonon) and turn right to reach the village of Essert-la-Pierre where vehicles are left (alt. 940 m).

Ascent: Left of the church, take the good track signposted to the Col de Tavaneuse which climbs up through the forest. The slope is steep right from the start until you reach the first pastures. While climbing up through the forest, ignore first of all the track on the right for the Pointe de Nantaux, then the one which leads to the Chalets de la Croix, and finally also the one that leads to the Chalets de la Chaux. The Chalets de Céraucez are reached at the exit from the wooded section (alt. 1,440 m). Leave the good track at the last bend before the chalets and continue upwards on a well marked path to the last of the chalets (Brion, alt. 1,650 m). From this point one has a very clear view of the elongated summit of Tavaneuse, situated on the right of the crest which overlooks the chalets. Further right, beyond the Col de Tavaneuse, the very slender Pointe de Nantaux towers up. To the right of the chalets, for a hundred metres follow a path which, by a long traverse, leads to the Col de Tavaneuse. Then leave this path and, aiming to the left, climb a grassy slope devoid of tracks, so as to reach the crest right of a little round shaped col. Follow the crest to the right on good tracks as far as the foot of the lower summit rise. Go along the foot of this briefly to the right and climb the third couloir on the left and then you can easily reach the summit.

Descent: Follow the opposite slope (south-east) as far as the Col de Tavaneuse. Then, slanting away from the summit and going downwards, return to the Chalets de Brion on the Col de Tavaneuse path mentioned above. Finally rejoin the ascent route.

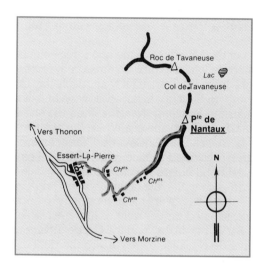

08   Pointe de Nantaux

- height: 2,170 m
- starting point: Morzine
- route: from the south-west
- grade: I
- climbing time: 3 hours 30 minutes
- views: very beautiful
- type of ground: woodland, grass
- IGN map: 3528 ET – 1:25 000   Didier Richard No 3 – 1:50 000

Access: At Morzine, take the road for Thonon-les-Bains and follow it for about 3 km as far as the bridge at Plagnettes. Continue several hundred metres (still towards Thonon) and turn right to reach the village of Essert-La-Pierre where vehicles can be left (alt. 940 m).

Ascent: Left of the church, take the path signposted to the Col de Tavaneuse. A little higher up, leave this path and take another on the right signposted to the Pointe de Nantaux. This climbs up through the forest and passes a large chalet (holiday camp). Further on, leave this path and take another on the right and stay on it. In places the tracks are more or less obvious. Pass in front of a chalet, then two others in ruins and finally an ancient cowshed. At the end of the wooded section, pass another ruined cowshed and at this point head directly to the left towards the crest. Go past some fir trees as well as a small barn and approach the grassy crest. Ascend this, passing near a last group of ruined huts on the right and continue to the summit (with a cross) which is reached after a final exposed section.

Descent: Descend by the same route.

Route notes

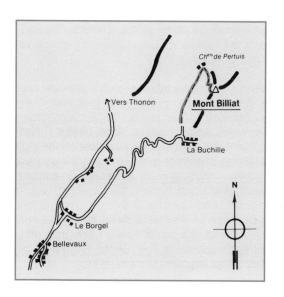

09 Mont Billiat

- height: 1,895 m
- starting point: Bellevaux, 23 km south of Thonon-les-Bains
- route: from the west
- grade: I
- climbing time: 2 hours
- views: very beautiful
- type of ground: grass
- IGN map: 3428 ET – 1:25 000   Didier Richard No 3 – 1:50 000

Access: From Thonon-les-Bains, take the D26 to the outskirts of Bellevaux and, 1 km before the village, take a road on the left signposted to Le Borgel-La Buchille. Follow it as far as the last zig-zag before the chalets at La Buchille, i.e. practically at the end of the road. Leave vehicles by this sharp bend (alt. 1,440 m).

Ascent: At the bend, take a good track on the left along the base of the Montagne du Pleiney leading to the Chalets de Pertuis (alt. 1,586 m). From the chalets, climb a large grassy slope on the right, following the left hand edge. At the top of the slope, take a fairly steep rise to the right and via a fault on the left enter a sort of cirque dominated at its head by Mont Billiat. Negotiate a series of zig-zags and, via a traverse to the right, reach the summit crest. Follow this to the left to reach the peak.

Descent: Descend by the same route.

Route notes

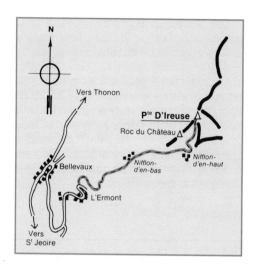

10   Pointe d'Ireuse

- height: 1,891 m
- starting point: Bellevaux, 23 km south of Thonon-les-Bains
- route: from the south-west
- grade: I
- climbing time: 2 hours 30 minutes
- views: beautiful
- type of ground: woodland, grass
- IGN map: 3428 ET – 1:25 000   Didier Richard No 3 – 1:50 000

Access: From Thonon-les-Bains, take the D26 to the village of Bellevaux. Behind the church, take the small road which leads to L'Ermont where vehicles can be left (alt. 1,010 m).

Ascent: At the beginning of L'Ermont, by a signpost, take a motor road on the left and immediately afterwards a path on the right which rises through the pastures beside a fence. A little higher up, aim to the right and enter the forest where the path rises in steep zig-zags. At the end of the wooded part, cross a grassy slope to a flat area where there is a potholing club hut and the Chalets de Nifflon-d'en-Bas. By the cross situated near the chalets, turn off to the right in the direction of some fir trees and, after some semi-wooded, semi-grassy sections, reach the Chalets de Nifflon-d'en-Haut (private hut). Descend into the hollow where there is a small chapel and ascend the couloir situated on the flank of the Roc du Château (easy rocks, tracks). By going to the right, reach the base of the summit block, keeping at the same level, then turn off left to scramble up to the summit cairn.

Descent: Descend by the same route.

Route notes

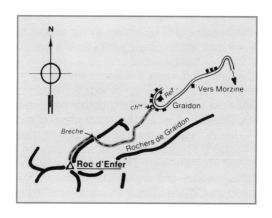

11 Roc d'Enfer

- height: 2,244 m
- starting point: Morzine
- route: from the south-east
- grade: II
- climbing time: 3 hours
- views: very beautiful
- type of ground: grass, stones
- equipment necessary: rope
- IGN map: 3528 ET – 1:25 000   Didier Richard No 3 – 1:50 000
  Graidon Hut (CAF)
  no warden Tel: 50 79 04 91

Access: At Morzine, take the D28 which leads to Gets and leave it after about 1 km to take a road on the right signposted to Thonon. Leave this several hundred metres further on, at the hamlet of Granges, and go round left towards Essert-Romand. Immediately after passing the road to Côte-d'Arbroz, turn left again to the hamlet of Gaydons, on the small road which leads very steeply up to Graidon. Leave vehicles near the chapel (alt. 1,425 m).

Ascent: Behind the chapel, take a good path which ascends a small, slightly inclined valley, dominated on the left by a long rock barrier (Rochers de Graidon). Go to the head of the valley and straight ahead climb a steeper slope which leads to a big flat area. From this flat area, turn off slightly to the right and, via a short traverse, reach the bottom of a valley full of rocks and dominated on the right by the long, exposed crest of the Roc d'Enfer. Climb the left side of the valley a little way and make a traverse to the right in the direction of a very obvious gap which splits the crest (way-marks and red arrows on the rocks). Reach the gap after a short ascent. From this point on, the route requires the greatest prudence. Start along the narrow and exposed ridge to the left and follow it as far as the first summit. Continue beyond this to the second point which constitutes the main summit. It is between these two points that the ascent is at its most exposed, so do not hesitate to rope up. Although this route is exposed, there is no technical difficulty.

Descent: It is imperative that descent be made by the same route.

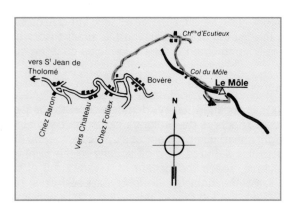

12   Le Mole

- height: 1,863 m
- starting point: Saint-Jean-de-Tholomé, 11 km north of Bonneville
- route: from the north-west
- grade: I
- climbing time: 2 hours 30 minutes
- views: very beautiful
- type of ground: woodland, grass
- IGN map: 3429 ET – 1:25 000   Didier Richard No 3 – 1:50 000

Access: From Bonneville, follow the N203 for about 1.5 km in the direction of Annemasse and then turn right on to the D12. Go through Faucigny and a bit further on turn right on to the D20 to Saint-Jean-de-Tholomé. Continue on towards Bovère, passing the hamlets of Chez Baron, Vers Chateau and Chez Folliex. After this last hamlet, turn left and stop a little higher up at the first bend (alt. 980 m).

Ascent: From the bend, where one can leave vehicles, a small wooden hut is visible about 50 metres uphill in the meadow. Take the grassy track which leads to it and continue on the good, broad path beyond. Higher up, climb a slope in the forest, fairly steep in places, to reach the Chalets d'Ecutieux. Heading southwards on good tracks all the time, reach the Col du Môle (high tension pylon). Continue beyond the col and climb a grassy slope (path practically non-existent) as far as a sort of flat area. From there one can go directly to the summit by following the path which rises in front of you up a very steep and tiresome slope. It is preferable to traverse to the right and to join up with another well marked path which contours the summit and allows one to reach it from the other side.

Descent: Descend by the same route.

Route notes

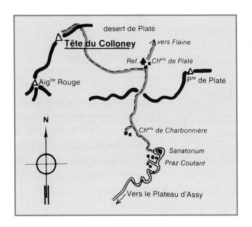

13   Tête du Colloney

- height: 2,692 m
- starting point: Passy, 5 km east of Sallanches
- route: from the south
- grade: II
- climbing time: 4 hours 30 minutes
- views: magnificent
- type of ground: woodland, stones
- IGN map: 3530 ET – 1:25 000   Didier Richard No 3 – 1:50 000
- Platé Hut (CAF)
  hut warden   Tel: 50 93 11 07

Access: From either Sallanches or Le Fayet, go to the village of Passy. Take the D43 and follow it as far as the Plateau d'Assy. Carry on climbing about 3 km up to Praz-Coutant (alt. 1,200 m). Leave vehicles at the end of the road, above the last houses and near the sanatorium.

Ascent: Take the broad track straight ahead leading to the Chalets de Charbonnière. On approaching these chalets, leave the track and head to the right on a well marked path which rises in zig-zags towards the imposing rocky barrier which dominates the Plateau d'Assy. The slope is steep but the path is well constructed. Close to the face, keep level with a rocky tower on the left so as to reach behind it a large chimney full of scree. Climb this (very steep) and on the left get on to a long flat ledge (exposed) cut in the rock which enables one to emerge on to the upper plateau called Désert de Platé. The Platé Hut is reached in a few minutes (alt. 2,032 m) and is surrounded by some chalets. A spring rises behind the hut, your last water supply. From this point on, one is recommended not to wander from the route and to follow the red painted discs on the rocks meticulously. Start off well to the left in a natural channel between the rocks and then go up a grassy slope towards the right. Higher up, cross several rocky crevasses and make for the crest blocking the horizon. The summit of Le Colloney, which has a trig point, lies to the left along this crest, separated from it by a gap. Reach the crest and continue along it as far as the gap and then cross it with care (tricky section). From the gap, ascend a boulder-field, then some easy rocks and reach the summit after a short exposed section. This route is marked with red arrows all the way.

Descent: Descend by the same route.

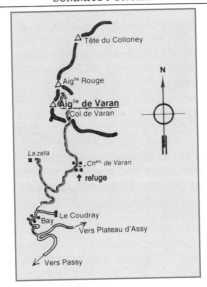

14 Aiguille de Varan

- height: 2,541 m
- starting point: Passy, 5 km east of Sallanches
- route: from the east
- grade: II
- climbing time: 3 hours 30 minutes
- views: magnificent
- type of ground: woodland, grass, stones, rocks
- equipment necessary: rope
- IGN map: 3530 ET – 1:25 000   Didier Richard No 3 – 1:50 000
- Varan Hut (private)
  hut warden   Tel: 50 93 61 98

Access: From either Sallanches or Le Fayet, go to the village of Passy and take the D43 which leads to the Plateau d'Assy. At a bend 4 km beyond Passy, turn left towards Bay-le-Coudray. On arrival in Bay, leave vehicles at the top of the village (alt. 1,100 m).

Ascent: Uphill from Bay, beyond the last houses, take the broad track towards the Chalets de Varan. A little higher up, ignore another track on the left which leads to La Zéta. Reach the Chalets de Varan (alt. 1,630 m), situated on a small plateau. From the chalets, take a path on the left, marked with red arrows, which rises through a wide valley and heads towards a long rocky crest running west-east, which starts from the Aiguille de Varan to the west. At first the slope is grassy but rapidly becomes stony and steep. At the top of the valley, cross the crest at the Col de Varan. The Aiguille de Varan is the first summit to the left of the col. It is immediately followed on the right by the very slender and vertical Aiguille Rouge. Make for the crest separating these two needle point peaks through a maze of rocks. Some large cairns here and there indicate the route. Exit on to the crest at a gap from where the view down the other side is impressive. At this spot the vertical face plunges towards the valley of the Arve. Leave the gap on the left, following the crest, and reach the foot of the summit block. Continue southwards to the end of a grassy ledge. Then head to the right up the rock and climb a chimney (good holds). Traverse about 10 metres right and climb a second chimney on the left (good holds) which emerges on to the very exposed summit.

Descent: Descend by the same route.

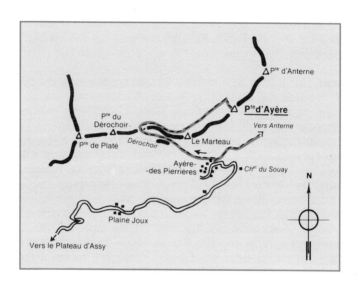

15 Pointe d'Ayère

- height: 2,641 m
- starting point: Passy, 5 km east of Sallanches
- route: from the north-west
- grade: III
- climbing time: 4 hours 30 minutes
- views: magnificent
- type of ground: stones, rocks
- equipment necessary: rope
- IGN map: 3530 ET – 1:25 000   Didier Richard No 3 – 1:50 000

Access: From either Sallanches or Le Fayet, go to the village of Passy. Take the D43 and follow it as far as the Plateau d'Assy, then continue to Plaine-Joux. Continue eastwards beyond Plaine-Joux on a little road suitable for motors which becomes less so in the vicinity of the Chalets du Souay. However, it is possible to follow it to its end by the Chalets d'Ayère-des-Pierrières (alt. 1,650 m).

Ascent: Having arrived in Ayère-des-Pierrières, ignore the path on the right (which goes to the Col d'Anterne) and, by the side of the spring, traverse the meadow north-westwards. Very quickly one finds a good path way-marked with red painted discs. Head towards the base of the vertical face of Le Marteau, the upper part of which consists of an enormous overhang, well visible from the start. Walk along this face towards the west and, above a small rough gorge, reach the foot of the wall level with a broad crack equipped with chains and cables. This section is called the Dérochoir and is the only way up. Cross the face here and emerge on to the crest. Follow the very exposed narrow crest to the right and descend as far as a gap (tricky section). Ascend the other side on a grass slope, then progressively move away from the crest into the maze of a slabby boulder slope and enormous rocks. Without losing height, make a big traverse in the direction of the base of the long rocky face of Nord-Ouest d'Ayère. Pass first below a large scree couloir surmounted by smooth slabs (the ridge has collapsed at this point). Continue as far as a concave part of the face, in the form of an almost complete circle, with a small couloir at the bottom. There is usually some snow here. Ascend this concave section towards the left and get into a small rocky couloir which splits the wall. A third of the way up the couloir, traverse 15 metres to the right (the traverse is obvious) and get into a second, parallel couloir. Climb to the top of it and exit by a short fairly steep chimney (good holds). Above this the summit cairn is quickly reached.

Descent: It is imperative that descent be made by the same route.

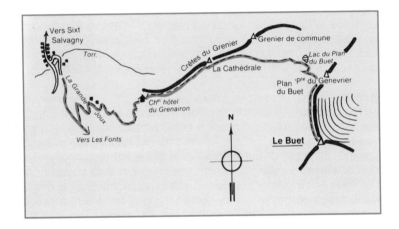

16 Mont Buet

- height: 3,094 m
- starting point: Sixt, 27 km east of Cluses
- route: from the north-west
- grade: II
- climbing time: 1st day: 2 hours 30 minutes; 2nd day: 4 hours
- views: magnificent
- type of ground: woodland, stones, snow
- equipment necessary: rope, ice axe
- IGN map: 3530 ET – 1:25 000   Didier Richard No 3 – 1:50 000
- hut: Chalet Hôtel du Buet Grenairon (private)
  hut warden   Tel: 50 34 47 31

Access: At Cluses, take the N202 to Taninges and the N507 to Sixt. Cross the River Giffre and follow a small road for about 2 km, as far as the hamlet of Salvagny. Turn left immediately after the last houses and leave vehicles at the end of the surfaced part of the little road (alt. 1,950 m).

Ascent:

First day: Straight ahead, follow the good road (arrows) which leads to the Chalets des Fonts but do not go that far. Break off shortly after starting to take the road on the left to Grenairon, which rises in zig-zags through the dense forest of La Grande Joux. The ascent is long and can seem monotonous. At the end of the wooded part, emerge on to a flat area at the Chalet Hôtel du Grenairon (alt. 1,950 m). From here the view of the west flank of the Buet is striking. The hotel, open and wardened during the summer, is provided with individual bedrooms as well as dormitories. Meals are available. Spend the night here.

Second day: Climb up behind the hotel on a stony slope to reach the Crêtes du Grenier, a long rocky ridge which runs towards the north-east. Turn right and follow the line of the ridge. The path threads its way through a rocky maze amongst curious limestone towers, one of which strangely resembles a church and is called La Cathédrale (alt. 2,498 m). Continue moving more to the east and head towards the vast Plan du Buet in front of the long ridge between the Pointe du Genévrier on the left and the Buet on the right. Traverse the Plan du Buet, pass to the right of a small lake and climb an unstable slope which gives access to the crest at a depression to the right of the Pointe du Genévrier. From here on be careful, roping up if necessary. On the right, attack the north ridge of the Buet, fairly exposed, vertical on each side and made up of flaky limestone schists. If the slope is wet, be doubly careful, for a slip could have grave consequences. High up on the ridge, reach the summit section, which is often very snowed up, and follow it, keeping to the left, thus reaching the culminating point, which is provided with a view indicator.

Descent: It is imperative that descent be made by the same route.

2. AIGUILLES ROUGES

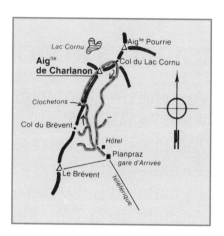

17   Aiguille de Charlanon

- height: 2,549 m
- starting point: Chamonix
- route: from the south
- grade: I
- climbing time: 2 hours 30 minutes
- views: magnificent
- type of ground: stones, rocks
- IGN map: 3630 OT – 1:25 000   Didier Richard No 8 – 1:50 000

Access: In Chamonix, take the Brévent téléférique as far as Planpraz (enquire about times of departure and return. Basically, in July and August the first car leaves at 7 a.m.; during the first half of September at 8 a.m.. Buy return tickets).

Ascent: At Planpraz (alt. 2,000 m) climb up behind the téléférique station on good tracks. A little higher up ignore the first path which leads to Lac Cornu and La Charlanon, for this is not the route which is used for our ascent. Take the second path just above on the right, signposted to Clocher and Clochetons de Planpraz. Further on, ignore the path on the left for the Col du Brévent and, after a steep climb up scree and rocks, reach the base of the Clochetons de Planpraz. Pass behind these and aim to the right towards the ridge which is reached via a small couloir on the left. Follow the broad and easy crest north-eastwards, sometimes on the top, sometimes below it. The attractive looking summit is thus easily reached from this side.

Descent: Descend on the far side of the summit to a gap (short tricky section) which allows one to reach the east-north-east ridge made up of big blocks. Immediately after the gap, go round a small rocky tower on the right and descend the easy ridge as far as the Col du Lac Cornu. Then turn off smartly to the right (southwards) towards the base of the Charlanon and return to Planpraz without any problem.

Route notes

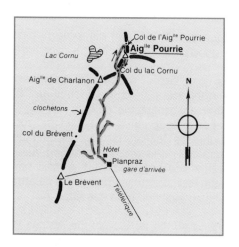

18   Aiguille Pourrie

- height: 2,562 m
- starting point: Chamonix
- route: from the south
- grade: I
- climbing time: 2 hours 30 minutes
- views: magnificent
- type of ground: stones, rocks
- IGN map: 3630 OT – 1:25 000   Didier Richard No 8 – 1:50 000

Access: In Chamonix take the Brévent téléférique as far as Planpraz (enquire about times of departure and return. Basically, in July and August the first car leaves at 7 a.m.; during the first half of September at 8 a.m.. Buy return tickets).

Ascent: At Planpraz (alt. 2,000 m) climb up behind the téléférique station on good tracks and a little higher up take a path on the right signposted to Lac Cornu. Further on ignore the path on the right, which leads to La Flégère, and by a long ascending traverse (northwards), well below the Clochetons de Planpraz and the Aiguille de Charlanon, reach the Col du Lac Cornu (alt. 2,406 m), situated between the Aiguille de Charlanon on the left and the Aiguille Pourrie on the right. Cross the col in order to walk along the opposite slope (Lac Cornu is visible below). Do not descend but follow the yellow painted discs on the rocks to the right and, by a short traverse (north-eastwards), reach the Col de l'Aiguille Pourrie (alt. 2,459 m). Do not continue on the tracks which lead further northwards towards the Lacs Noirs. Turn right towards the south and climb the easy rocky ridge which gives access to the summit.

Descent: Cross the summit and descend the southern ridge, taking care always to keep Lac Cornu in sight on the right. This will bring you back to the Col du Lac Cornu and thence to Planpraz by the route followed on ascent.

Route notes

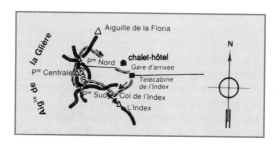

19　Aiguille de la Glière - North Summit

- height: 2,846 m
- starting point: Chamonix
- route: from the east
- grade: II
- climbing time: 3 hours
- views: magnificent
- type of ground: stones, rocks, snow
- equipment necessary: rope, ice axe
- IGN map: 3630 OT – 1:25 000　　Didier Richard No 8 – 1:50 000
- hut: Chalet Hôtel de la Flégère (private)
  hut warden　Tel: 50 53 06 13

Access: At Praz de Chamonix, take the Flégère téléférique, then the Index télécabine (enquire about times of departure and return. Basically, in July and August the first car leaves at 7 a.m.; during the first half of September at 8 a.m.. Buy return tickets).

Ascent: From the upper station of the Index télécabine (alt. 2,390 m), take the Index path. Ascend the steep boulder field which leads to the Col de l'Index, situated between the Aiguille de l'Index on the left and the south-east ridge of the Aiguille de la Glière on the right. Reach the Col de l'Index (alt. 2,549 m), then turn right and climb a small easy wall (good holds), in order to set foot on the south-east ridge of the Glière. Follow the rocky ridge which presents no difficulty. Having arrived at a flat area, one comes up against the sudden rise of the south summit which one needs to go round to the right. Emerge on to a large hanging, fairly steep snowfield and ascend it on the left, so as to reach the knife-edge ridge. This section can be tricky if the snow is very hard and one is recommended to use rope and ice axe in such conditions. Continue along the ridge towards the central summit (alt. 2,852 m), a practically vertical tower. At its base, go round to the left of it and rejoin the ridge. This leads quickly to the north summit.

Descent: Cross the summit and descend the north-east ridge (be sure to take the more northerly right hand ridge, that on the left must be avoided). At the level of a flat area, below the summit, work your way down a basin full of scree on the Chamonix side and rejoin the upper station of the télécabine at the bottom of the basin.

Route notes

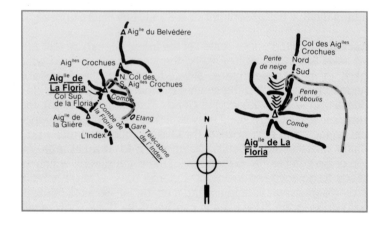

20 Aiguille de la Floria

- height: 2,888 m
- starting point: Chamonix
- route: from the north-east
- grade: III
- climbing time: 3 hours
- views: magnificent
- type of ground: stones, rocks, snow or ice
- equipment necessary: rope, ice axe, crampons
- IGN map: 3630 OT – 1:25 000   Didier Richard No 8 – 1:50 000
- hut: Chalet Hôtel de la Flégère (private)
  hut warden   Tel: 50 53 06 13

Note: This route is best done at the start of the season when it provides a beautiful stretch of snow from the Col des Aiguilles Crochues to the summit of the Aiguille de la Floria. At the end of the season the north-east ridge is bare and tricky.

Access: At Praz de Chamonix, take the Flégère téléférique, then the Index télécabine (enquire about times of departure and return. Basically, in July and August the first car leaves at 7 a.m.; during the first half of September at 8 a.m.. Buy return tickets).

Ascent: From the Index télécabine station (alt. 2,390 m), face towards the Aiguilles Rouges and then traverse an area of big rocks. Very soon a path appears which ascends northwards. A little further on, ignore the path on the left which heads towards the Floria valley and follow a long moraine. Continue northwards, passing close by a pond and, after having crossed the base of a rocky spur, arrive at the foot of a large basin parallel to that of the Floria. Traverse this low down and, beyond the spur which borders its left bank, leave the path and attack the steep scree slope on the left leading to the crest. Via a fairly easy rocky couloir, reach the crest at the southern Col des Aiguilles Crochues, a narrow gap which gives access to the north-west slope. At precisely this point one must put on crampons and rope up. Cross the col on to the opposite slope and immediately move to the left. Climb the steep snow or ice slope which borders the north-east ridge of the Aiguille de la Floria and high up on this slope (very steep exit) rejoin the ridge on the left above its main rise. Then follow the fairly steep ridge to the summit.

Descent: It is possible to cross the summit and return via the ordinary route down the south-west ridge and the Col Supérieur de la Floria. However, it is advisable to descend by the same route, especially if the route is done at the start of the season, for the north-east ridge is then generally well covered in snow.

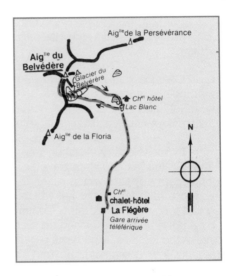

21 Aiguille du Belvédère

- height: 2,966 m
- starting point: Chamonix
- route: from the east
- grade: II
- climbing time: 3 hours 30 minutes
- views: magnificent
- type of ground: stones, rocks, snow
- equipment necessary: rope, ice axe
- IGN map: 3630 OT– 1:25 000   Didier Richard No 8– 1:50 000
- hut: Chalet Hôtel de la Flégère (private)
  hut warden   Tel: 50 53 06 13

Access: At Praz de Chamonix take the Flégère téléférique (enquire about times of departure and return. Basically, in July and August the first car leaves at 7 a.m.; during the first half of September at 8 a.m.. Buy return tickets).

Ascent: At the upper téléférique station (alt. 1,930 m), take the good path (arrows) on the right which leads to the Lac Blanc. The ascent is easy in a splendid setting. Reach the Lac Blanc (alt. 2,354 m), situated on a small plateau. The Aiguille du Belvédère, culminating point of the Aiguilles Rouges range, dominates the Lac Blanc with its imposing mass and thus is unmistakable. The lake consists of two small areas of water and is fed by the torrent which flows from the Glacier du Belvédère. Start on the left and go uphill from the first pool, by the chalet-hotel, and climb a rocky promontory which forms the true right bank of the basin (left side when ascending) where the Belvédère torrent flows. The path is more or less well marked but climb in a straight line in the direction of the crest to reach the Glacier du Belvédère which is no more than an easily inclined snow slope. Reach the south ridge of the Belvédère at its lowest point (left of the summit). Follow the ridge to the right and climb the easy rocks. Ascend a vaguely defined chimney couloir (exposed but easy, good holds) and emerge on to the big shoulder which leads quickly to the summit.

Descent: From the base of the south ridge, descend the whole of the Glacier du Belvédère on the left hand side and rejoin the Lac Blanc via the scree basin.

Route notes

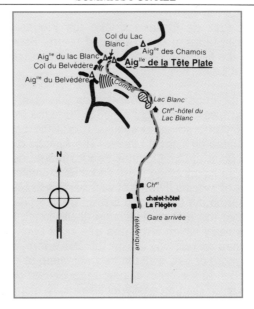

22 Aiguille de la Tête Plate

- height: 2,944 m
- starting point: Chamonix
- route: from the south-west
- grade: III
- climbing time: 4 hours
- views: magnificent
- type of ground: stones, rocks
- equipment necessary: rope, crampons, ice axe
- IGN map: 3630 OT– 1:25 000   Didier Richard No 8– 1:50 000
- hut: Chalet Hôtel de la Flégère (private)
  hut warden   Tel: 50 53 06 13

Access: At Praz de Chamonix, take the Flégère téléférique (enquire about times of departure and return. Basically, in July and August the first car leaves at 7 a.m.; during the first half of September at 8 a.m.. Buy return tickets).

Ascent: From the upper téléférique station (alt. 1,930 m), take the good path (arrows) on the right which leads to the Lac Blanc. The ascent is easy in a splendid setting. Reach the Lac Blanc (alt 2,354 m), situated on a small plateau, at the foot of the Aiguille du Belvédère and at the bottom of a large basin. Ascend this basin north-westwards in the direction of the Col du Belvédère which separates the Aiguille du Belvédère on the left from the Aiguille du Lac Blanc on the right. Do not go as far as the col; two-thirds of the way up the basin, head right towards a steep couloir covered with snow, situated just after the main couloir which ends up at the Col du Lac Blanc, a small col separating the aiguilles Lac Blanc and Tête Plate. Climb the couloir (crampons and ice axe useful) and, halfway up, climb the rocks on the right (good holds), so as to get into the main Col du Lac Blanc couloir. Ascend the couloir until level with a groove on the right and a little below the col. Climb this steep groove fairly easily and emerge on to the summit of the Tête Plate, which is obviously higher than the Aiguille du Lac Blanc.

Descent: Descend by the same route. Do not stray from the path.

Route notes

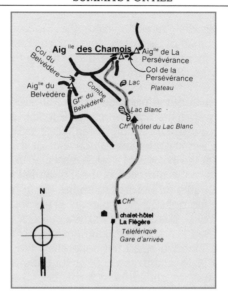

23 Aiguille des Chamois

- height: 2,902 m
- starting point: Chamonix
- route: from the south
- grade: III
- climbing time: 4 hours
- views: magnificent
- type of ground: stones, rocks
- equipment necessary: rope, ice axe
- IGN map: 3630 OT–1:25 000   Didier Richard No 8–1:50 000
- hut: Chalet Hôtel de la Flégère (private)
  hut warden   Tel: 50 53 06 13

Access: At Praz de Chamonix, take the Flégère téléférique (enquire about times of departure and return. Basically, in July and August the first car leaves at 7 a.m.; during the first half of September at 8 a.m.. Buy return tickets).

Ascent: At the upper téléférique station (alt. 1,930 m) take the good path (arrows) on the right which leads in about 1 hour 30 minutes to the Lac Blanc (alt. 2,354 m). Looking northwards from the lake, and not far from it, one can make out very clearly the Aiguille de la Persévérance, the most slender of all those visible in this sector. The Aiguille de Chamois is situated just to the left of the Persévérance and separated from it by the Col de la Persévérance (alt. 2,840 m). Ignore the large basin on the left which descends from the Col du Belvédère as far as the Lac Blanc and ascend northwards amongst the glacier polished rocks mixed with grass or snow. However, as soon as the Lac Blanc hut is no longer visible and one has reached the plateau situated at the foot of the aiguilles, aim to the left towards the wall. Pass close by a small lake, then climb obliquely to the right up a large scree slope often covered in snow, located between the Pointes de Beugeant on the left and a rocky spur descending from the Chamois on the right. The top of the slope, now very steep, narrows and abuts against the south ridge of the Chamois at the point where it loses itself in the headwall. At this level, climb an easy sort of chimney couloir on the left on unstable rocks and reach a small gap which gives a view of the Bérard slope. Descend 2 metres on this slope via a chimney couloir, then move right to the very exposed west-south-west ridge. Follow this as far as the summit, going round the rocks.

Descent: It is imperative to descend by the same route.

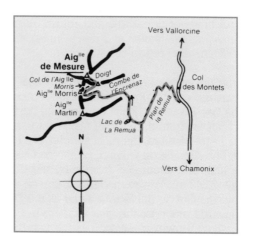

24 Aiguille de Mesure

- height: 2,812 m
- starting point: Argentière, 8 km north of Chamonix
- route: from the east
- grade: III
- climbing time: 4 hours 30 minutes
- views: magnificent
- type of ground: stones, rocks
- equipment necessary: rope
- IGN map: 3630 OT – 1:25 000   Didier Richard No 8 – 1:50 000
- hut: Gîte Rural La Boerne à Trélechamps (private) hut warden   Tel: 50 54 05 14

Access: From Chamonix via the N506, Praz and Argentière, drive to the Col des Montets (alt. 1,461 m) where vehicles can be left.

Ascent: At the col, take the path on the left signposted to the Lac Blanc and follow it as far as the Plan de la Remua, a vast flat area reached via a long series of zig-zags. Leave the path and head right across the little stone walls towards a large couloir with a mixture of grass and rock. Ascend this (some tracks) and emerge at the little Lac de la Remua (alt. 2,162 m) situated on a flat area. Traverse off to the right to reach a knoll topped by a signal. Continue upwards amongst rocks and enter the valley of l'Encrenaz. Ascend this as far as the level of a conspicuous scree cone situated to the right of and at the base of large slabs. Climb right up the centre of this steep slope of grassy scree, then cross an easy short rocky section (good holds) on the left. Aim to the left and climb above the great slabs by a sort of couloir full of grass and rocks. At the top of the couloir, climb a small 3-metre wall (tricky but on good holds). Continue above it for a short distance, turn right and traverse as far as the couloir of the Col de l'Aiguille Morris which one reaches practically at the level of the col (alt. 2,707 m). Ascend towards the col and aim to the right in the direction of the east ridge of the Aiguille de Mesure, following a fairly easy course but made up of split rocks, marked by cairns. Reach the ridge to the left of the Doigt de Mesure, a beautiful slender aiguille on the same ridge, and climb the easy large rocks which lead to the summit of the Aiguille de Mesure.

Descent: It is imperative that descent be made by the same route.

Route notes

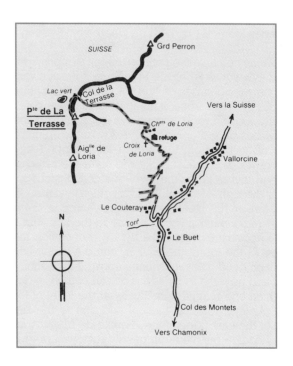

25 Pointe de la Terrasse

- height: 2,734 m (Chaîne des Perrons)
- starting point: Vallorcine, 16 km north of Chamonix
- route: from the east
- grade: I
- climbing time: 4 hours

> views: magnificent
> type of ground: woodland, grass, stones
> IGN map: 3630 OT– 1:25 000   Didier Richard No 8– 1:50 000
> Hut Chalet de Loria (private)
> hut warden   Tel: 50 54 06 45

Access: From Chamonix via the N506, Argentière and the Col des Montets, drive to the hamlet of Buet. Continue towards Vallorcine for about 1 km only and take a small road on the left signposted to Couteray. A little further on, ignore a road on the right, then another on the left. (Follow the signs to Loria). Go as far as the end of the road, near the last houses, at the entrance to the forest (alt. 1,400 m).

Ascent: Follow the track straight ahead and leave it after the first big hairpin to take a good path on the right signposted to Loria and climb up through dense forest. A little higher up, ignore the Tré-les-Eaux/Les Granges path on the left and emerge on to a forest track. Follow this to the right for a few moments and leave it at the first bend to rejoin the Loria path. After the wooded section, the Loria cross is reached and a little higher up the Chalets de Loria, situated on a small open plateau (alt. 2,020 m). A private hut provides accommodation and meals. Climb above the chalets, westwards, following the red way-marks. Ascend a vast valley enclosed by the frontier hill crest. The Pointe de la Terrasse lies to the left of the valley and the Col de la Terrasse splits the crest at the top. Climb as far as the col via a steep scree slope (hard going). To the left of the col, climb some easy rocks and follow the broad, slightly inclined crest to the summit.

Descent: Descend by the same route.

3. ■ BORNES

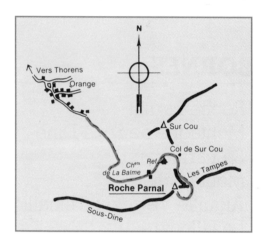

26 Roche Parnal

- height: 1,896 m
- starting point: Thorens, 19 km north-east of Annecy
- route: from the north-west
- grade: I
- climbing time: 3 hours
- views: very beautiful
- type of ground: woodland, grass, stones
- IGN map: 3430 ET – 1:25 000   Didier Richard No 2 – 1:50 000
- Balme Hut (CAF)
  no warden

Access: At Annecy, take the N203 in the direction of Bonneville and follow it as far as Groisy-le-Plot where you turn right on to the D2 to Thorens. Continue on the D2 towards Roche-sur-Foron and turn off right 7 km further on to reach Orange. Leave vehicles at the top of the hamlet at the end of the motor road by the signpost to the Chalets de la Balme (alt. 1,160 m).

Ascent: Take the good track straight ahead which ascends a wooded slope to the Chalets de la Balme (alt. 1,500 m), situated on a small plateau at the foot of the Roche Parnal, the east flank of which consists of an almost vertical rocky face. Continue eastwards, soon reaching the small CAF hut tucked away in a wood of fir trees. Further on, one emerges on to the Col de Sur Cou, situated not far above the hut. Then aim to the right, so as to contour the base of the Roche Parnal. Ascend a small, very steep couloir, which lies between the rocks of Les Tampes on the left and the Roche Parnal on the right, to a little col. Briefly contour the Roche Parnal once more, so as to get to its less intimidating south-east flank. Climb this to the right via a succession of grassy terraces to the summit.

Descent: Descend by the same route.

Route notes

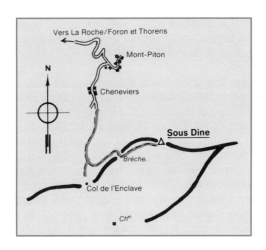

27 Montagne de Sous-Dine

- height: 2,004 m
- starting point: Thorens, 19 km north-east of Annecy
- route: from the north-west
- grade: I
- climbing time: 3 hours
- views: very beautiful
- type of ground: woodland, grass, stones
- IGN map: 3430 ET – 1:25 000   Didier Richard No 2 – 1:50 000

Access: At Annecy, take the N203 in the direction of Bonneville and follow it as far as Groisy-le-Plot where one turns right on to the D2 for Thorens. Continue on the D2 towards Roche-sur-Foron and turn off right 6 km further on towards Mont-Piton. Turn right again to get to the hamlet of Cheneviers. Leave vehicles beyond the asphalted portion of the road (alt. 1,100 m).

Ascent: Take the track straight ahead which rises through a dense forest. A little further on (about 15 min), ignore another very steep track on the left. Then ignore a track on the right which leads to the Col de l'Enclave. On arriving at a clearing, the rocky escarpments of Sous-Dine are visible to the right. Keep traversing eastwards through the forest. Suddenly the track comes to an end and one has the impression of not being able to go any further; however, the track becomes a path. Follow it, then climb to the right and, via a series of broad zig-zags, reach the foot of the face, level with a depression offering a way upwards. Climb the steep slope of this depression and exit above by a gap. Beyond here the tracks are practically non-existent, so take a bearing on the summit to the left. Look for a way across grass and rock, firstly on the left, then on the right, and on to the end.

Descent: Descend by the same route. Do not wander about, especially between the summit and the gap. Do not look for another way down through the rocky barrier other than by this gap (Danger!)

Route notes

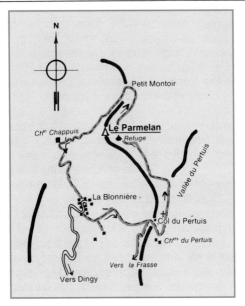

28   Le Parmelan - complete traverse

- height: 1,832 m
- starting point: Dingy-Saint-Clair, 12 km east of Annecy
- route: from the south-west
- grade: I
- climbing time: 3 hours 30 minutes
- views: very beautiful
- type of ground: woodland, grass, stones, rocks
- IGN map: 3430 ET – 1:25 000   Didier Richard No 2 – 1:50 000
- Parmelan Hut (CAF)
  hut warden   Tel: 50 27 29 45

Access: From Annecy via the D5 and the D16 as far as the bridge at Saint-Clair, then on the D216 to Dingy-Saint-Clair. At the top of the village, take the little road which leads to Blonnière (alt. 950 m).

Ascent: At the bend before the first of the houses, by the signpost to Blonnière, take a track on the right between two chalets which ascends eastwards. A little further on, ignore a track on the right which leads to the Chalet du Crêt Riant. Aim to the left to pass by the Chalets des Fournets (alt. 1,000 m), then above turn right and climb a series of steep, zig-zags in the forest. At the end of the wooded section, ignore a path on the right which descends to La Frasse. Via easy rocks and a couloir, reach the Col du Pertuis (alt. 1,565 m) which splits the long rocky barrier. On the other side of the col, pass quite close to the Chalets des Pertuis (alt. 1,582 m, situated on a pasture, and go round a grassy knoll on the right. The well marked path leads north-north-west following the line of the rocky Parmelan crest. Pass a cross erected in memory of a forester who died in a snow storm. Higher up ascend a boulder field on the left, then cross a sort of easy chimney couloir. Continue to traverse the fairly steep slabby boulder slope. Traverse several hollows, avoiding a number of more or less deep holes. Emerge on to the upper plateau and reach the hut which marks the top of the climb.

Descent: Below and to the right of the hut, take a path which leads northwards and round the end of the rocky Parmelan crest. At the level of the Petit Montoir, turn to the south-west and walk along the base of the rocks to the Chalet Chappuis. Take care not to take the wrong path; look for the signpost to the chalet; and from there carry on to Blonnière.

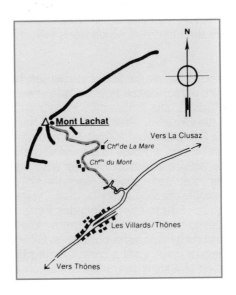

29 Mont Lachat

- height: 2,020 m
- starting point: Les Villards-sur-Thônes, 24 km east of Annecy
- route: from the south-east
- grade: I
- climbing time: 2 hours 30 minutes
- views: beautiful
- type of ground: grass, stones, rocks
- IGN map: 3430 ET – 1:25 000   Didier Richard No 2 – 1:50 000

Access: From Annecy on the N509, through Thônes to Villards-sur-Thônes. Continue in the direction of La Clusaz for about 1.5 km, then turn left (facing a sawmill) and follow a small road as far as a junction (signposted left to Plan des Villards). Leave vehicles at this junction (alt. 850 m).

Ascent: Take the path which rises northwards up a grassy slope. Pass three chalets in succession and enter a forest. Above the short wooded section, pass a fourth chalet, then climb another grassy slope which leads to the Chalets du Mont (alt. 1,217 m). Continue above the chalets, then aim to the right to emerge on to a small plateau (Chalet de la Mare). Go round immediately to the left and, keeping always northwards, ascend a fairly bushy slope to reach the surroundings of an enormous boulder field, situated below the crest of Mont Lachat. Climb this towards the left as far as a rocky area which one crosses on the right. Emerge on to the narrow summit surmounted by a large metal cross.

Descent: Descend by the same route.

Route notes

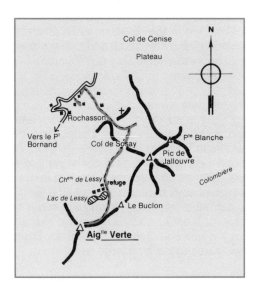

30   Aiguille Verte du Chinaillon

- height: 2,045 m
- starting point: Le Petit-Bornand, 12 km south of Bonne-ville
- route: from the north
- grade: I
- climbing time: 3 hours
- views: beautiful
- type of ground: grass, stones
- IGN map: 3430 ET – 1:25000   Didier Richard No 2 – 1:50000
- Lessy Hut (private)
  hut warden   Tel: 50 25 98 32

Access: From Bonneville on the D12 to the village of Petit-Bornand. Behind the town hall, take the road for the Plateau de Cenise which rises through the forest. Higher up, ignore the road to Paradis on the right. Continue beyond the asphalted section through the mountain pastures. Pass a group of chalets and above, where the slope steepens immediately after a right hand bend, leave vehicles on the left at the side of the road by an ancient quarry (alt. 1,500 m).

Ascent: Follow briefly the little gravelled road which goes through a copse of fir trees. Ignore the first path on the right which leads to some chalets (large cross). Also avoid the second and take the third on the right, which traverses the pastures. Pass a ruined chalet, then another and finally the last two which are joined together. Continuing to traverse, head towards a broad gap in the mountain, dominated by the Pic de Jallouvre. Ascend a short slope bordered on the left by a ravine and, crossing the gap, emerge into a cirque. Go slightly left for a few moments, then go round right to climb a boulder field which leads to the Col de Sosay, situated to the right of the Jallouvre (climber's right facing the col). From the col the small Lac de Lessy and its chalets are visible to the south, as well as the Aiguille Verte du Chinaillon at the end of the ridge. Descend to the lake and take the path on its left which joins the ridge between the Buclon and the Aiguille Verte. Follow the ridge to the right to the summit.

Descent: Descend by the same route.

Route notes

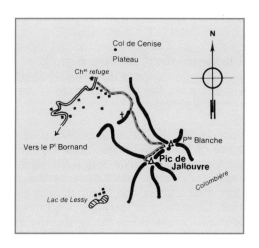

31   Le Jallouvre

- height: 2,408 m
- starting point: Le Petit-Bornand, 12 km south of Bonne-ville
- route: from the north-west
- grade: II
- climbing time: 3 hours
- views: very beautiful
- type of ground: grass, stones, rocks
- IGN map: 3430 ET – 1:25 000   Didier Richard No 2 – 1:50 000
- Cenise Hut (private)
  hut warden   Tel: 50 03 51 39

Access: From Bonneville on the D12 to the village of Petit-Bornand. Behind the town hall, take the road to the Plateau de Cenise and follow it to its end (partly metalled) if your vehicle will take the last steep part of the slope. The end of the road is on a level with a chalet-hut (alt. 1,600 m).

Ascent: From this point do not continue to climb towards the Col de Cenise but start directly to the right (eastwards) across pastures, so as to join the path which heads towards the foot of the long north-west crest of the Pointe Blanche (on the climber's left when ascending). Between this ridge and a little eminence on the right, flanked by a cross, negotiate an easy rise provided with iron railings to reach a cirque. Climb to the left into the heart of the cirque along a boulder field which descends from the Col du Jallouvre. Traverse the upper part of the boulder field to reach the col (striking view of the Colombière slope). Carefully tackle on the right hand side the section known as the 'Rasoir' which consitutes the knife-edge part of the Col du Jallouvre, a short but exposed passage. Continue contouring the summit of the Jallouvre westwards via the section called the 'Cravate' (feeling of exposure, no difficulty, but keep moving). Then coming back to the left, climb the easy rocks which give access to the summit.

Descent: Descend by the same route.

Route notes

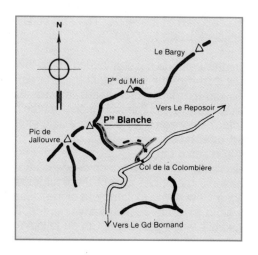

32 Pointe Blanche

- height: 2,437 m
- starting point: Le Grand-Bornand, 32 km east of Annecy
- route: from the south-east
- grade: I
- climbing time: 3 hours
- views: very beautiful
- type of ground: grass, stones, rocks
- IGN map: 3430 ET – 1:25 000   Didier Richard No 2 – 1:50 000

Access: From Annecy via the N509 and Thônes to the village of Grand-Bornand. Continue on up to the Col de la Colombière. Leave vehicles on the car park at the col (alt. 1,613 m).

Ascent: Take the good path which rises above the hotel on the Col de la Colombière and rapidly reach a large mountain chalet. Fifty metres further on the track forks. Take the left fork and go around a knoll on the right. At this spot the path is barely marked on the grassy slope. Head towards a large rock on the right. when you reach the same height, aim to the left and make an ascending traverse as far as a small rocky barrier on the right. Continue as far as a boulder field which descends along a rocky spur. Ascend the boulder field, then higher up attack the rocky face on the left and climb it easily. Emerge on to the ridge from where one has a fine view of the large valley on the left which descends from the Col du Jallouvre. Ascend the ridge and reach the summit via a series of steep zig-zags.

Descent: Descend by the same route.

Route notes

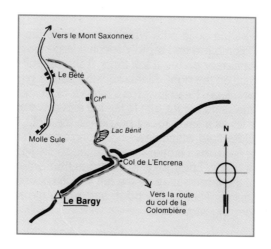

33   Le Bargy

- height: 2,299 m
- starting point: Mont-Saxonnex, 11 km east of Bonneville
- route: from the north-west
- grade: I
- climbing time: 3 hours
- views: very beautiful
- type of ground: grass, stones, rocks
- IGN map: 3430 ET – 1:25 000   Didier Richard No 2 – 1:50 000

Access: Between Bonneville and Cluses, at Marnaz, take the D286 and follow it as far as Mont-Saxonnex. At the top of the village turn left into the little road which leads to Morsullaz and go as far as the hamlet of Bété where vehicles can be left (alt. 1,156 m).

Ascent: Start along the good track (arrows) on the left signposted to Lac Bénit. The slope is gentle and a large flat area is rapidly reached from which one can see the imposing north face of Le Bargy, made up of impressive slabs and dièdres. The track descends a hundred or so metres to Lac Bénit (alt. 1,450 m), lying at the foot of Le Bargy. Level with the lake, the face is deeply cut and a broad scree couloir gives access to the Col d'Encrena. Go around the lake to the right to the bottom of the couloir, then climb the steep stony slope by a well marked path. Higher up, climb a tricky section on a rocky nose (good holds), then traverse the couloir to the left (tricky) to reach the Col d'Encrena (alt. 1,990 m). To the right of the col, climb the easy rocks and reach the crest which is followed to the top. Watch out for the numerous holes, some of which are several metres deep.

Descent: Descend by the same route. However, it is possible to descend the opposite side of the peak by a well marked path from the Col d'Encrena, past the Chalets de la Cha, Malatrait and Saint-Bruno (alt. 1,237 m), down to the road which climbs up from Reposoir to the Col de la Colombière. For this it is necessary to leave a vehicle on this side.

Route notes

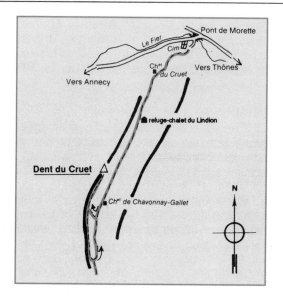

34 Dent du Cruet

- height: 1,833 m
- starting point: La Balme de Thuy, 17 km east of Annecy
- route: from the east
- grade: I
- climbing time: 3 hours 30 minutes
- views: beautiful
- type of ground: woodland, grass, stones
- IGN map: 3431 OT–1:25 000   Didier Richard No 2–1:50 000
- Lindion Hut (private)
  hut warden   Tel: 50 02 08 34

Access: At Annecy, take the N509 in the direction of Thônes and follow it as far as the military cemetery at Morette just before the bridge which crosses the River Fier (Commune of La Balme de Thuy). Between the cemetery and the bridge, take a road suitable for motor vehicles on the right which ends a little further on. Follow it to the end where vehicles can be left (alt. 580 m).

Ascent: Take a good path straight ahead which rises in steep zig-zags through the forest. Higher up, pass the Chalets du Cruet (alt. 864 m), then the Chalet du Lindion (alt. 1,123 m). Continue southwards through a small valley alongside the long crest on the right, headed by the Dent du Cruet. Having reached the Chalet de Chavonnay-Gallet, continue briefly up the valley until a subsidence in the crest on the right is visible, producing a sort of natural hollow in the slope. Leave the path at this point and tackle the slope on the right, half grass, half stones and totally devoid of tracks, in the direction of the crest, following the right hand edge of this hollow. Emerge on to the crest and follow it to the right as far as the summit.

Descent: Descend by the same route, or from the summit retrace your steps and follow the crest to its southern end, then turn left and get back to the Chalet de Chavonnay-Gallet in the valley (advised).

Route notes

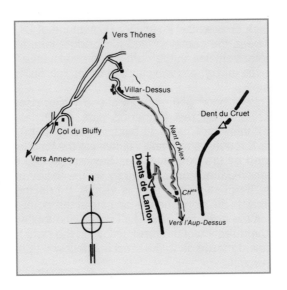

35 Dents de Lanfon

- height: 1,824 m
- starting point: Bluffy, Col de Bluffy, 10 km east of Annecy
- route: from the east
- grade: II
- climbing time: 3 hours 30 minutes
- views: very beautiful
- type of ground: woodland, stones, rocks
- IGN map: 3431 OT – 1:25 000   Didier Richard No 2 – 1:50 000

Access: At Annecy, take the N509 in the direction of Thônes. About 1 km after the Col de Bluffy, turn right and go to the hamlet of Villar-Dessus. Immediately after the spring, turn left (footpath sign to L'Aup) and go as far as the end of the road where vehicles can be left in a car park (alt. 800 m).

Ascent: Take the fairly steep path on the right of the car park which rises through the forest alongside the Nant d'Alex stream. Go as far as the Chalets de l'Aup-Riant-Dessous (alt. 1,443 m), situated at the entrance to a little valley between the Grandes Lanches on the left and the Dents de Lanfon on the right. The path ascends the valley but leave it at this point. Turn right in front of the chalets and make your way on good tracks towards the imposing rocky mass at the foot of the Dents de Lanfon. Walk along the face towards the right as far as its end and start to contour it. Suddenly the well marked path turns left and by a series of zig-zags reaches the bottom of a very steep, stony couloir which should be climbed with care (beware stonefall!). Pass close by a cave situated near the top of the couloir on the left. Higher up, when approaching the crest, traverse left, then cross two easy rocky sections, the second of which has a fixed cable. Do not be tempted by the good tracks which lead off right at several points towards the crest. Keep on the level and go round rocks and holes and reach the narrow summit which is steep and exposed.

Descent: It is imperative that descent be made by the same route. It is dangerous to wander about. (Danger!)

Route notes

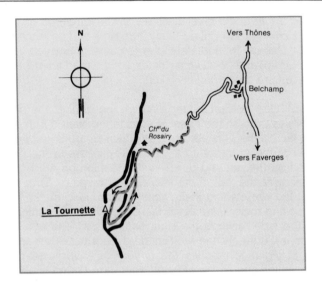

36   La Tournette - East side

- height: 2,351 m
- starting point: Thônes, 20 km east of
  Annecy
- route: from the north-east
- grade: I
- climbing time: 3 hours 30 minutes
- views: very beautiful
- type of ground: woodland, grass, stones
- IGN map: 3431 OT – 1:25 000   Didier Richard No 2 – 1:50 000
- Chalet du Rosairy Hut
  hut warden

Access: From Annecy, take the N509 to Thônes. On the right of the church, take the D12 in the direction of Faverges and follow it for about 3 km as far as the locality of Belchamp, situated immediately after the bridge over the River Chamfroid. Turn right on to the little road signposted to La Tournette and leave vehicles on a small car park at the end (alt. 1,046 m).

Ascent: Above the road, take the good path which rises through the wood in a succession of zig-zags. Emerge on to the mountain pasture and carry on to the Rosairy Hut (alt. 1,645 m). Continue above the hut, turning completely left to follow the base of a long rocky barrier. Walk along with this on your right as far as the level of a couloir which splits it. Ascend the fairly steep couloir and high up aim to the left in the direction of the monolith which marks the top. Go round this on the south side and climb a steep chimney provided with cables, steps and an iron ladder. Thus you can easily reach the summit.

Descent: At the bottom of the chimney, follow the base of the crest southwards and reach the top of a broad couloir to your left. Descend this and walk along the base of the rocky barrier. This brings you back to the Rosairy Hut. Continue down the way you came up.

Route notes

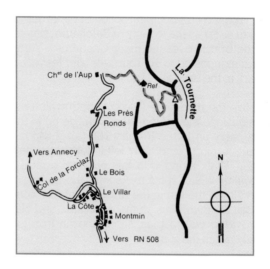

37   La Tournete - West side

- height: 2,351 m
- starting point: Montmin, Col de la Forclaz, 22 km south-east of Annecy
- route: from the west
- grade: I
- climbing time: 3 hours 30 minutes
- views: very beautiful
- type of ground: grass, stones, rocks
- IGN map: 3431 OT– 1:25 000   Didier Richard No 2– 1:50 000
- Tournette or Blonay-Dufour Hut (private)
  hut warden   Tel: 50 68 98 41

Access: At Annecy, take the N509 running along the eastern shore of the lake, then the N509A which is left just before the descent to Talloires where you turn left on to the D42. Follow this as far as the Col de la Forclaz. Descending towards Montmin, about 2 km after the col turn left and, via a fairly narrow little mountain road, reach the flat area by the Chalet de l'Aup de Montmin (alt. 1,420 m).

Ascent: Ascend a steep, grassy slope to the right of the chalet facing the imposing hill face which crowns the top of La Tournette. Reach the first rocky spurs of the mountain on good tracks. Follow the path which winds to the right and arrive at the Tournette Hut (alt. 1,850 m), situated in a cirque. Descend slightly left below the hut, then on the right continue towards the head of the cirque. Then turn off to the left and climb up a stony slope facing the rock wall, so as to reach an upper plateau which allows one to contour the top of the cirque leftwards. Make a long ascending traverse northwards. At the end, aim to the right and by a good path cut into the rock, reach the crest, just to the left of the final rise called the 'Fauteuil' (armchair). Contour round this last 30-metre high obstacle on the left (eastern side) and climb it by a steep chimney equipped with steps, cables and an iron ladder.

Descent: Descend by the same route.

Route notes

38 Crêt des Mouches

- height: 2,032 m
- starting point: Saint-Ferréol, 28 km south-east of Annecy
- route: from the east
- grade: I
- climbing time: 3 hours 30 minutes
- views: very beautiful
- type of ground: woodland, grass
- IGN map: 3431 OT– 1:25 000   Didier Richard No 2– 1:50 000

Access: At Faverges (N508 Annecy-Ugine), take the D12 in the direction of Thônes to the village of Saint-Ferréol. Continue along the D12 for about 1.5 km and take a little road on the left towards La Côte. Pass through this hamlet and drive to the end of the road in the vicinity of Le Fontany (alt. 800 m).

Ascent: Cross the pastures straight ahead to reach the path on the right which starts between two rows of trees. Climb up through a not very dense forest for about an hour to the Chalet Plan-du-Chouet (alt. 1,209 m), situated in a clearing. After passing the chalet, climb a little slope on the left, so as to reread the path which goes through the forest. After a series of zig-zags, leave the wooded area. Aim to the right in the direction of the rocky base, pass by the side of a ruined cowshed set in a hollow and ascend a grassy slope to a bare crest. Pass a sign indicating the site of a spring and traverse another wooded section. Level with the base of the rocks, traverse a boulder field and contour round the Pointe de Chauriande on its eastern side. Then head northwards to the Chalets d'Arclosan situated in a hollow. On the right ascend a grassy slope and emerge on to the crest. Turn left along the crest in order to reach the summit, on which stands a cross.

Descent: Descend by the same route.

Route notes

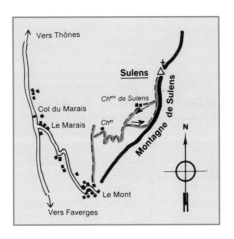

39   Montagne de Sulens

- height: 1,839 m
- starting point: Serraval, Col du Marais, 30 km south-east of Annecy
- route: from the south-west
- grade: I
- climbing time: 2 hours
- views: very beautiful
- type of ground: grass
- IGN map: 3531 OT – 1:25 000   Didier Richard No 2 – 1:50 000

Access: From Annecy on the N509 to Thônes and the D12 to the Col du Marais. On a small road to the left, go as far as the hamlet of Le Mont where vehicles can be left by the last houses (alt. 1,100 m).

Ascent: Left of the road, take a good track signposted to Sulens-les-Bancs. Follow this northwards where it leads through a wood. Not far from the start (about 15 min), ignore the first track on the right, then a second a little higher up where the ground levels out. A hundred metres after this second track, take a path on the right to reach a large alpine chalet (alt. 1,300 m). Then aim to the right and, by a series of zig-zags up a fairly steep slope, go through a small wood. Move to the left while traversing, then again to the right (eastwards) up a second fairly steep slope. Emerge on to the long, ridge-pole crest and follow it briefly below the top on the left. Finally straddle it northwards as far as the cross which marks the end.

Descent: Descend by the same route. It is equally possible to return via the Chalets de Sulens, situated below the west face. From the chalets, traverse southwards to rejoin the ascent path.

Route notes

4. ARAVIS

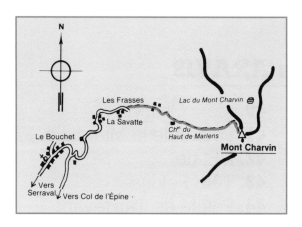

40 Mont Charvin

- height: 2,407 m
- starting point: Le Bouchet, 34 km south-east of Annecy
- route: from the west
- grade: I
- climbing time: 3 hours 30 minutes
- views: very beautiful
- type of ground: grass, stones
- IGN map: 3531 OT – 1:25 000   Didier Richard No 8 – 1:50 000

Access: From Annecy on the N509 to Thônes, then the D12 to Serraval and the D162 to the village of Bouchet-Mont-Charvin. Continue in the direction of the Col de l'Epine for less than 1 km and take a little road on the left which leads to the hamlet of La Savatte, at the end of the asphalted road. Continue on the metalled road past the fork to the hamlet of Les Frasses. Leave vehicles not far from there, by the path which starts on the left (alt. 1,250 m).

Ascent: Uphill from the hamlet of Les Frasses, take the broad path on the left, signposted to Charvin, which rises through the pastures. Higher up, on approaching a group of chalets, ignore a path on the right which heads southwards. Pass between the chalets and continue on the path as far as the Chalet du Haut de Marlens (alt. 1,657 m), behind a mountain hut. Above the chalet, follow the tracks along an electric fence, heading towards a valley coming down from Mont Charvin. At the top of the pastures, take a well marked path and ascend it eastwards. Cross a stream, then climb the steep boulder field in the valley and, via a series of zig-zags, emerge on to the knife-edge ridge left of the summit. Follow this ridge to the right as far as the fairly exposed top.

Descent: Descend by the same route.

Route notes

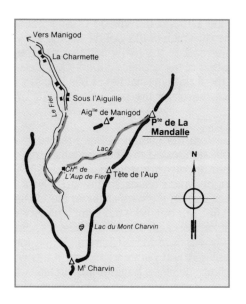

41 Pointe de la Mandalle

- height: 2,277 m
- starting point: Manigod, 26 km east of Annecy
- route: from the west
- grade: I
- climbing time: 3 hours 30 minutes
- views: very beautiful
- type of ground: woodland, grass
- IGN map: 3531 OT – 1:25 000   Didier Richard No 8 – 1:50 000

Access: From Annecy on the N509 to Thônes, then the D16 to Manigod. In the direction of the Col de la Croix-Fry, after the church in Manigod village, take the little Tournance road on the right and follow it to its end in the vicinity of Sous-l'Aiguille (alt. 1,158 m). Leave vehicles in the car park.

Ascent: Take the steep, stony path straight ahead which rises beside the River Fier through a forest of fir trees. After a series of zig-zags, emerge into a vast valley, dominated on the right in its upper part by Mont Charvin. To the left the Aiguille de Manigod is visible, flanked by two crosses and a large mountain chalet. Level with a ruin, abandon the path which ascends the valley and take another on the left, so as to reach the chalet. Continue beyond this (eastwards, then north-eastwards) on good tracks as far as a small lake bordered by ruins. At this point the path is not clear, so aim a little to the left and, by a series of small valleys, come to an open plateau, sited between the Aiguille de Manigod on the left and the long crest which joins the Charvin and the Pointe de la Mandalle on the right. Clamber up to the crest and follow it to the left to reach the summit.

Descent: Descend by the same route.

Route notes

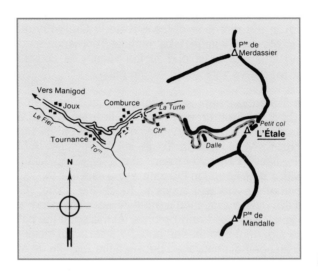

42 L'Etale

- height: 2,484 m
- starting point: Manigod, 26 km east of Annecy
- route: from the west
- grade: II
- climbing time: 4 hours
- views: very beautiful
- type of ground: woodland, grass, stones
- equipment necessary: rope
- IGN map: 3531 OT – 1:25 000   Didier Richard No 8 – 1:50 000

Access: From Annecy on the N509 to Thônes and the D16 in the direction of the Col de la Croix-Fry, to Manigod. In the village, take the little road to Tournance on the right and leave it just after the hamlet of Joux, to take another on the left, signposted to Comburce. Follow this as far as it is suitable for motors to a car park (alt. 1,200 m).

Ascent: To the right of the car park, take a path signposted to L'Etale and cross a stream. Pass the first big mountain chalet and climb an open slope as far as the Chalet de la Turte (alt. 1,364 m). Cross a forest road and ascend a steep, wooded slope. Aim to the right below a rocky barrier and, making a long sweep around to the left, reach the bottom of a couloir where a large slab ends (well indicated with blue marks). Climb the couloir and get out of it to the right beside the slab (tricky). After a steep couloir-chimney, emerge on to a vast slope of grass and rocks and ascend it as far as a ledge (spring) from whence the summit signal is visible. Now aim slightly left and ascend a boulder field. Traverse this upwards and to the left and then climb a steep slope of mixed grass and stones (tricky section to start with). Head towards a very steep couloir and ascend it as far as a small col. Move to the right (blue arrow) up the final steep and exposed slope with extreme care (very tricky but well provided with aids) to the summit.

Descent: It is imperative that descent be made by the same route.

Route notes

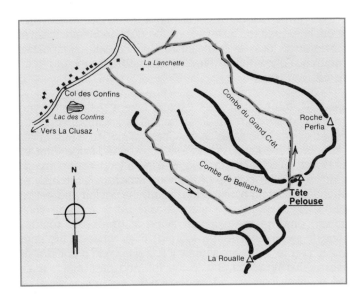

43 | Tête Pelouse

- height: 2,539 m
- starting point: La Clusaz, 31 km east of Annecy
- route: from the north-west
- grade: I
- climbing time: 3 hours
- views: very beautiful
- type of ground: stones
- IGN map: 3430 ET – 1:25 000   Didier Richard No 8 – 1:50 000

Access: From Annecy, on the N509 via Thônes to La Clusaz, then take the Confins road alongside the Aravis range and follow it as far as the Col des Confins (alt. 1,470 m). Leave vehicles on the level ground at the col.

Ascent: The summit of Tête Pelouse is situated at the end of the long rocky crest which borders the lefthand side of the Combe de Bella Cha. It is your goal. Level with the last houses, head right across meadows and reach the foot of the Combe de Bella Cha which dominates the Col des Confins. First of all, walk through a wood of fir trees on the left, then a little higher up turn to the right and head towards the centre of the valley. Ascend by a series of steep zig-zags and follow a slight ridge in the middle of the valley. This brings you to a good flat area (alt. approximately 2,150 m) where the valley bends to the left. At this point resist the desire to keep going straight ahead. Aim to the left and climb the last part of the fairly hemmed-in valley. Just before the top of the valley, reach a rocky ridge on the left and follow it to the right to the summit.

Descent: Descend by the same route. It is equally possible, and indeed it is recommended, to descend by the following route: from the summit, descend to the bottom of the short ridge at the point where you started up it. Drop over to the right into the Combe du Grand Crêt, parallel to that of the Bella Cha and descend it right down to the mountain pasture of La Lanchette. Take a broad track on the left to rejoin the Col des Confins.

Route notes

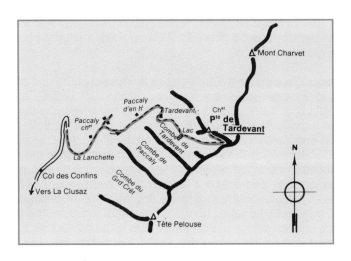

44　Pointe de Tardevant

- height: 2,500 m
- starting point: La Clusaz, 31 km east of Annecy
- route: from the north-west
- grade: I
- climbing time: 3 hours
- views: very beautiful
- type of ground: stones
- IGN map: 3430 ET – 1:25 000　　Didier Richard No 8 – 1:50 000

Access: From Annecy via the N509 and Thônes to La Clusaz, then take the Confins road which runs beside the Aravis range and follow it as far as the Col des Confins (alt. 1,470 m). Leave vehicles on the level ground at the col.

Ascent: From the col, take the good track straight ahead and in 15 minutes reach the mountain pasture of La Lanchette, situated at the foot of the Combe du Grand Crêt (first valley after the Col des Confins). Continue on the broad path parallel to the range without ascending. After the first chalet on the left, you need to leave the path. Just before the Chalets de Paccaly (alt.1,459m) at the bottom of the Combe de Paccaly, which is next to that of the Grand Cret, leave the path which leads to the Pointe Percée and take another path on the right which heads towards the Combe de Paccaly. Ascend it a short distance and traverse to the other slope. Ignore a path on the right which leads to Trou de la Mouche and pass the Chalet de Paccaly-d'en-Haut (alt. 1,673 m). A little further on, enter the Combe de Tardevant and ascend it on good tracks. Pass the Chalet de Tardevant (alt. 1,805 m), then the Lac de Tardevant (alt. 2,118 m). Above here the tracks are less obvious, so ascend aiming to the left towards a sort of small, slightly inclined valley which is ascended by its left flank to reach the crest. Turn left and follow the crest to the exposed summit point.

Descent: Descend by the same route.

Route notes

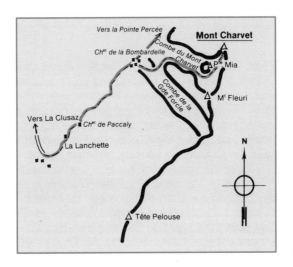

45   Mont Charvet

- height: 2,539 m
- starting point: La Clusaz, 31 km east of Annecy
- route: from the north-west
- grade: II
- climbing time: 4 hours
- views: very beautiful
- type of ground: woodland, stones, rocks
- IGN map: 3430 ET – 1:25 000   Didier Richard No 8 – 1:50 000

Access: From Annecy via the N509 and Thônes to La Clusaz, then take the Confins road which runs alongside the Aravis range and follow it to the Col des Confins (alt. 1,470 m). Leave vehicles on the level ground at the col.

Ascent: From the col, take the good track straight ahead and in 15 minutes reach the mountain pasture of La Lanchette at the foot of the Combe du Grand Crêt (first valley after the Col des Confins). Continue on the good path which runs parallel to the range without trying to ascend. Pass the Chalets de Paccaly (alt. 1,459 m) and ignore the Paccaly valley on the right. Pass through a forest of fir trees. Ignore the path on the right which leads to Tardevant and reach the Chalets de la Bombardelle (alt. 1,601 m) at the bottom of the Combe de la Grande Forcle. To the right and in the direction of this valley, ascend a path which winds up a cleft splitting a great slab. Higher up the path, now less marked, veers left towards the neighbouring valley, that of Mont Charvet. To reach it pass close by the first of the rocks which separate the two valleys. Climb up, keeping to the right, without worrying about the non-existent path at this point. Attain the top of the valley which leads to a cirque dominated by the crest of Mont Fleuri. Here the path reappears on the left. Get on it and contour behind the Petite Mia, a rocky summit resembling a big molar tooth. Ascend a scree slope to emerge on to the level and aim to the right to reach the crest at its lowest point (alt. 2,404 m). Mont Charvet is to the left and is recognizable by its imposing rocky mass. Taking full precautions, ascend the rocky face, keeping as far as possible to the right. Below the summit, cross an easy steep chimney (good holds) to reach the cross marking the highest point.

Descent: Descend by the same route.

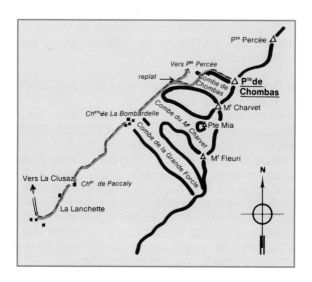

46 Pointe de Chombas

- height: 2,467 m
- starting point: La Clusaz, 31 km east of Annecy
- route: from the north-west
- grade: II
- climbing time: 4 hours
- views: very beautiful
- type of ground: woodland, stones
- equipment necessary: rope
- IGN map: 3430 ET– 1:25 000   Didier Richard No 8– 1:50 000

Access: From Annecy via the N509 and Thônes to La Clusaz, then take the Confins road which runs alongside the Aravis range and follow it to the Col des Confins (alt. 1470 m). Leave vehicles on the level ground at the col.

Ascent: From the col, take the good track straight ahead and in 15 minutes reach the mountain pasture of La Lanchette at the foot of the Combe du Grand Crêt (first valley after the Col des Confins). Continue on the good path which runs parallel to the range in the direction of the Pointe Percée without trying to ascend. Pass the Chalets de Paccaly (alt. 1,459 m) and ignore the Paccaly valley on the right. Pass through a wood of fir trees, ignore the path on the right which leads to Tardevant and arrive at the Chalets de la Bombardelle (alt. 1,601 m) at the bottom of the Grande Forcle valley. Beyond the chalets the path descends into a little hollow then ascends easily to reach good open, grassy level ground in front of a rocky area. From the flat area (alt. 1,620 m), one can make out the imposing rocky mass of Mont Charvet on the right. It is here that one turns off from the Pointe Percée path. Ascend to the right in the direction of the spurs of Mont Charvet. No path is discernible and it is necessary to trust to one's instinct in order to find the best way. On approaching the rocks, turn left and head towards the Combe de Chombas, situated between Mont Charvet and the Pointe de Chombas. Ascend the valley a little way, then make a rising traverse on the scarcely visible remains of an ancient path. Reach the other side of the valley, bordered by the long rocky crest descending from the Pointe de Chombas, at the height of a sort of promontory standing out from the crest. Climb this easily, keeping to the left and emerge on to the crest. Follow this to the right carefully, for it is very narrow for some metres, then cross an exposed section between two big blocks of rock. The crest then widens out and can be followed without further problem to the summit.

Descent: Descend by the same route.

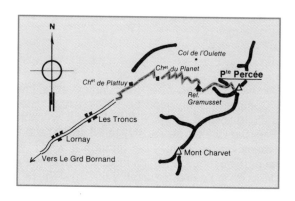

47   Pointe Percée

- height: 2,752 m
- starting point: Le Grand-Bornand, 31 km east of Annecy
- route: from the north-west
- grade: II
- climbing time: 4 hours
- views: magnificent
- type of ground: woodland, grass, stones, rocks
- equipment necessary: rope, ice axe
- IGN map: 3430 ET – 1:25 000   Didier Richard No 8 – 1:50 000
- Gramusset (Pointe Percée) Hut (CAF) hut warden   Tel: 50 02 40 90

Access: From Annecy via the N509 and Thônes to the village of Grand Bornand. Ignore the road on the left to the Col de la Colombière. Take the small road which runs alongside the River Borne and follow it to its end just after the hamlet of Troncs (car parking, alt 1,200 m).

Ascent: Continue straight ahead, taking a well marked path which rises through the forest to reach in about 45 minutes the Chalet de Plattuy (alt. 1,552 m), situated at the end of the wooded section. Immediately after passing the chalet, ignore a path on the left which leads to the Col des Annes. Continue up the small valley for a short distance, then turn off to the right to reach the Chalets du Planet (alt. 1,664 m). Go left around the chalets and behind them pick up the path coming up the valley and meet a little higher up on the level ground the path which comes from the Confins alongside the Aravis range. Turn off left, then further on tackle a long series of zig-zags on the right leading up to the Gramusset Hut (CAF, alt. 2,162 m). Here the Pointe Percée towers up imposingly above the hut with a forbidding aspect. Carry on uphill slightly to the left and make your way through a rocky maze, heading towards an obvious scree couloir often covered with snow, which splits the centre of the face. Ascend this couloir (fairly steep) and leave it halfway up to get on to the rocky section on the left which forms the outer base of the Pointe Percée (red way marks). Make your way into this rocky area and climb it (beware stonefall!) following the most convenient route. Ascend or traverse carefully a snowfield, the difficulty of which varies from year to year and head towards the crest dominating a concave section of the mountain in the line of ascent. Climb the terraces and emerge to the right of the narrow crest. The opposite slope is exposed. Follow the crest to the left and climb the final rise. Step across a broad cleft in the rock to reach the summit cairn.

Descent: It is imperative that descent should be by the same route.

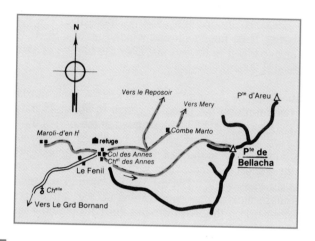

48   Pointe de Bella Cha

- height: 2,466 m
- starting point: Le Grand Bornand, 31 km east of Annecy
- route: from the north-west
- grade: II
- climbing time: 4 hours 30 minutes
- views: very beautiful
- type of ground: grass, stones
- equipment necessary: rope, ice axe
- IGN map: 3430 ET – 1:25 000   Didier Richard No 8 – 1:50 000
- Chalet la Cheminée Hut (private)
  hut warden   Tel: 50 27 03 87
- Chalet Frédéric Hut (private)
  hut warden   Tel: 50 27 01 37

Access: From Annecy via the N509 and Thônes to the village of Grand Bornand. Ignore the road to the Col de la Colombière on the left and follow the little road which runs alongside the River Borne as far as the hamlet of Les Plans. From there take another small road on the left signposted to La Duche and follow it to its end, the Col des Annes (alt. 1,722 m).

Ascent: Beyond the Col des Annes there is a large hollowed out valley parallel with the Aravis range giving access to Le Reposoir. On the right facing the range, take a path which traverses the top of the valley below the crest from which it stems. Thus reach the Aravis slope and head north towards a long grassy crest which plunges into the Combe du Reposoir and which is perpendicular to the neighbouring summits. The Pointe de Bella Cha is the highest point of this long crest. On the approach to it, traverse the bottom of a deep stony valley, then approach the crest along its length. Ascend the grassy section, keeping always to the left. When you come up against a rocky area, get into it and climb some easy terraces for some 20 to 30 metres, then traverse a little sloping corridor to the left to join a rocky ridge which is crossed at a very obvious fault. Ascend the ridge for a few metres, then when it rears up, go round it on the left (exposed but easy). The upper non-rocky section is fairly steep but can be climbed without problem. Cross the little terminal ridge, narrow, exposed and made up of unstable rocks to reach the summit.

Descent: Descend by the same route.

Route notes

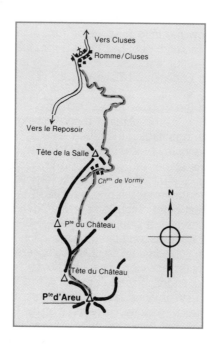

49   Pointe d'Areu

- height: 2,478 m
- starting point: Nancy-sur-Cluses, 4 km south of Cluses
- route: from the north
- grade: I

- climbing time: 4 hours
- views: very beautiful
- type of ground: woodland, grass, stones
- IGN map: 3430 ET– 1:25 000   Didier Richard No 8– 1:50 000

Access: At Cluses, take the D119 to Nancy-sur-Cluses. Continue to Romme (about 5.5 km above Nancy). Go right through the village and at the top of it turn left in the direction of Le Reposoir. Level with the last houses, leave vehicles by the side of the road (alt. 1,290 m).

Ascent: From the parking area, take a good track on the left alongside a ski lift, then enter the forest. After a series of broad and well designed zig-zags, which make the ascent much easier, emerge on to the pastures and ascend them southwards as far as the crest (views plunging down over toward the Arve valley). Aim to the right and contour around the Tête de la Salle to the left. Reach the Chalets de Vormy (alt. 1,903 m) on an open plateau, from where one can determine the correct route precisely. The Pointe d'Areu marks the end of the long crest which leads southwards and on which stand the intermediate summits of the Pointe du Château and the Tête du Château. Carry on directly southwards below the crest as far as a sort of shoulder which is ascended on the right. Reach the crest and follow it easily to the summit.

Descent: Descend by the same route.

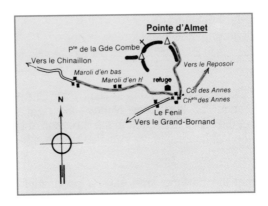

50   Pointe d'Almet

- height: 2,231 m
- starting point: Le Grand Bornand, 31 km east of Annecy
- route: from the south
- grade: I
- climbing time: 2 hours 30 minutes
- views: very beautiful
- type of ground: grass, stones
- IGN map: 3430 ET – 1:25 000   Didier Richard No 8 – 1:50 000
- Chalet de la Cheminée Hut (private)
  hut warden   Tel: 50 27 03 87
- Chalet Frédéric Hut (private)
  hut warden   Tel: 50 27 01 37

Access: From Annecy via the N509 and Thônes to the village of Grand Bornand, then take the road on the left to the Col de la Colombière as far as Chinaillon. Shortly after Chinaillon, still climbing up to the col, take a road suitable for motors on the right which passes the Chalets des Bouts and ends at the Chalets de Maroli-d'en-bas (alt. 1,578 m) where vehicles can be left.

Ascent: Continue on good tracks up a grassy slope to reach the Chalets de Maroli-d'en-Haut (alt. 1,731 m). Continue along the agreeably panoramic and relatively flat path to the Col des Annes (alt. 1,722 m) where there is a group of high mountain chalets. A small road which leads to the hamlet of Les Plans, east of Grand Bornand, comes up to the Col des Annes but this route is not recommended because the excursion is so short and because it cuts out the pleasant way from Maroli-d'en-bas to the Col des Annes. The Pointe d'Almet dominates the col to the left. Start off in this direction, following tracks leading towards a cirque dominated by a short narrow crest which joins the Pointe de la Grande Combe on the extreme left with the Pointe d'Almet on the extreme right. Do not ascend the cirque but aim to the right and climb a ridge. Below the summit, the ridge has a more steep and stony section. The peak is easily reached.

Descent: Descend by the same route.

Route notes

---

5. BAUGES

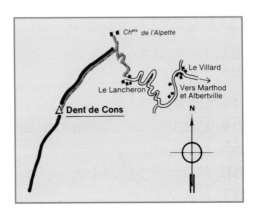

51 Dent de Cons

- height: 2,064 m
- starting point: Marthod (73), 6 km north of Albertville
- route: from the north-east
- grade: II
- climbing time: 3 hours
- views: very beautiful
- type of ground: woodland, grass, rocks
- IGN map: 3432 ET and 3531 OT – 1:25 000
  Didier Richard No 2 – 1:50 000

Access: From Albertville follow the N212 in the direction of Ugine for about 5 km, as far as the junction with the D103. Turn left on to this to Marthod. Go through the village and continue on to the hamlet of Le Lancheron at the end of the motor road. Leave vehicles on a car park (alt. 1,150 m).

Ascent: Take the broad path on the right which rises steadily as far as a sort of small col from where one can see below in a hollow the Chalets de l'Alpette (alt. 1,377 m). Do not go as far as the chalets but take a path on the left which climbs up through the forest. In places the path disappears but that poses no problem as the terrain allows no possibility of going astray. Emerge from the wooded section on to the open crest where good tracks reappear. Follow the exposed crest, cross a series of rises on easy rock, made tricky by the narrowness of the ridge and of the impressive steepness of the mountain. Continue to the summit cairn.

Descent: It is imperative to descend by the same route.

Route notes

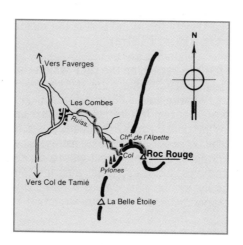

52 Le Roc Rouge

- height: 1,720 m
- starting point: Faverges, 26 km south of
  Annecy
- route: from the north-west
- grade: I
- climbing time: 3 hours 30 minutes
- views: very beautiful
- type of ground: woodland, grass
- IGN map: 3432 ET– 1:25 000   Didier Richard No 2– 1:50 000

Access: At Faverges take the D12 southwards towards the Col de Tamié and follow it for about 3 km and, immediately after passing the hamlet of Frontenex, turn left to Les Combes (alt. 1,877 m). Leave vehicles by the church.

Ascent: Follow the good track behind the church, uphill from the houses. Cross a road and further on cross a stream to the left and take a good path in front of you which climbs up through the forest. Higher up, ignore the path which breaks off to the left and continue to aim to the right, rejoining the stream at the point where a second stream comes in from the right. The spot is somewhat chaotic (rocks and torn up trees) and all tracks disappear. Cross the stream and, facing the mountain, ascend to the left of a small knoll situated at the junction of the two streams. Beyond the knoll, between two clumps of trees, the path reappears. The slope becomes more steep and the climb continues in a series of zig-zags. Cross the stream once more. Further on cross another stream. Keep climbing the very steep slope, ignore a path which breaks off to the right and, leaving the forest, reach the Col de l'Alpette to the left of three high tension pylons. Aim to the left, pass the Chalet de l'Alpette (alt. 1,580 m) from where the summit cross is visible and continue as far as the crest. Ascend this on the right (very exposed and dangerous) to reach the peak.

Descent: Descend by the same route

Route notes

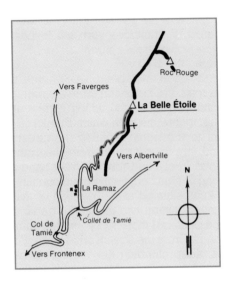

53   La Belle Etoile

- height: 1,841 m
- starting point: Mercury (73), 8 km west of Albertville
- route: from the south-west
- grade: I
- climbing time: 2 hours
- views: magnificent
- type of ground: woodland, grass
- IGN map: 3432 ET – 1:25 000   Didier Richard No 2 – 1:50 000

Access: At Albertville take the D104 and follow it beyond Mercury, as far as the Collet de Tamié, before the Col de Tamié. At the Collet de Tamié, take the little road on the right to La Ramaz and follow it to the end of the asphalted part, at the point where it becomes a private way, at a fork with a dirt road (alt. 1,100 m).

Ascent: Take a good path on the right (way-marked in orange) which climbs up through a dense forest. A little higher up (not far from the start) cross the private road which cuts across the path after a broad zig-zag. The tracks follow briefly the line of the road uphill, then climb an open slope. After a long series of steep zig-zags, leave the forest and reach the crest at the level of the first cross (alt. 1,710 m). From this point on, the route is really vertiginous and care is recommended. Follow the very narrow and exposed crest northwards as far as the summit, which is topped by a cross and a view indicator.

Descent: Descend by the same route.

Route notes

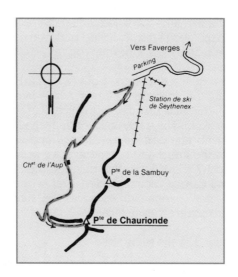

54   Pointe de Chaurionde

- height: 2,173 m
- starting point: Faverges, 26 km south of Annecy
- route: from the west
- grade: II
- climbing time: 3 hours 30 minutes
- views: very beautiful
- type of ground: woodland, grass
- IGN map: 3432 OT – 1:25 000   Didier Richard No 2 – 1:50 000

Access: At Faverges, take the D12 which leads to the Col de Tamié and follow it for 4 km, then turn right in the direction of Seythenex. At this village, take the forest road signposted to the ski station at Seythenex-la Sambuy. Go as far as the station which marks the end of the road. Vast car park at the foot of the ski lift (alt. 1,150 m).

Ascent: At the end of the car park, take a broad path on the left which rises through a forest of magnificent conifers (do not take the path which is a continuation of the car park and which descends towards the small valley of Saint-Ruph). After about 200 metres, ignore a large motor road on the left and continue right on the good path. The slope is gentle which makes for easy progress. Cross a wooden bridge over a stream and, after a short ascent, emerge on to a mountain pasture. Ascend a grassy slope leading to the Chalet de l'Aup de Seythenex (alt. 1,719m m), situated on a small plateau at the foot of the Sambuy. Turn to the east to face the Pointe de la Sambuy, so as to determine the position of the Pointe de Chaurionde. This is situated at the end of the crest to the right of the Sambuy. Follow the path past the chalet and head towards the bottom of a long crest which descends from the summit. Leave the path when it begins to descend towards the Col d'Orgeval, level with the bottom of the ridge. Get on to this ridge and follow faint tracks at the beginning which rapidly become a path. Follow the line of the ridge which rears up more and more to become a very steep grassy slope on the approach to the summit. Extreme care should be taken on this tricky section where a slip could have grave consequences. Although this final slope is very steep, it is nevertheless easy to climb, for it is provided with natural steps.

Descent: Descend by the same route.

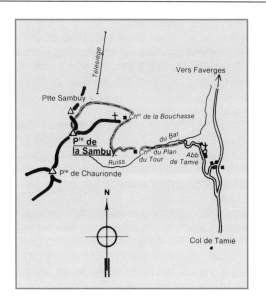

55   La Sambuy

- ■ height: 2,198 m
- ■ starting point: Faverges, 26 km south of Annecy
- ■ route: from the east
- ■ grade: I
- ■ climbing time: 3 hours 30 minutes
- ■ views: very beautiful
- ■ type of ground: woodland, stones
- ■ IGN map: 3432 OT and 3432 ET – 1:25 000 Didier Richard No 2 – 1:50 000

Access: At Faverges, take the D12 which leads to the Col de Tamié and, about 1.5 km before the col, at the hamlet of Pommarey, turn right to reach Tamié Abbey. Pass the abbey and a little further on, take a small forest road on the left and follow it to its end (alt. 1,050 m).

Ascent: Straight ahead, take the broad track which rises through a dense forest. From the start the slope is steep which makes no easier the approach to the Chalet du Plan du Tour (alt. 1,328 m), situated on level ground where the vegetation is dense. Turn right along the building. The path, faint at this point, disappears into a copse, crosses a dry stream bed, then climbs up again through the forest. The slope becomes painfully steep until you reach the end of the forest. Beyond the wooded section, make a big traverse to the right below a crest (the last water supply is in the middle of the traverse) and reach the Chalet de la Bouchasse (alt. 1,700 m), situated at the foot of a secondary summit topped by a cross. Contour around this to the right and enter a broad valley coming down from the Sambuy. On the right, the top of the chairlift coming up from Seythenex is visible. La Sambuy is situated at the top of the valley, to the left. The crest which descends to the right links up with the Petite Sambuy. Ascend the valley and head towards this crest, which is between the two Sambuy peaks. Continue leftwards in the direction of the nearby summit and reach it via its righthand flank. The final terraces can be tricky if the ground is damp.

Descent: Descend by the same route.

Route notes

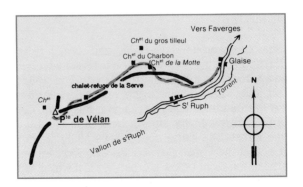

56   Pointe de Velan

- height: 1,783 m
- starting point: Faverges, 26 km south of Annecy
- route: from the east
- grade: I
- climbing time: 3 hours 30 minutes
- views: very beautiful
- type of ground: woodland, grass
- IGN map: 3432 OT – 1:25 000   Didier Richard No 2 – 1:50 000
- Chalet de la Serve Hut (private)
  hut warden   Tel: 50 44 50 25

Access: At Faverges, start on the D12 southwards towards the Col de Tamié in the direction of Seythenex (heavy goods road), then right again towards Villaret. Continue as far as Glaise, the second hamlet after Villaret. Leave vehicles near the spring (alt. 800 m).

Ascent: Ignore the small road which continues to Saint-Ruph and take a good path on the right which rises very steeply up the slopes of the Montagne de la Motte. Pass the Chalets de la Motte and du Charbon, near which one goes through an iron gate. Leaving the Chalets du Gros Tilleul off to the right (high tension pylon), go through a second gate to reach the Chalets de la Serve (alt. 1,441 m), situated on a small plateau. Beyond the line of the chalets the Pointe de Velan is visible, with a cross fixed on its top. Beside the chalets, take the beginnings of a path which contours to the right around a small knoll and fades out a little further on. Continue to the right along a trough and emerge on to level ground. Aim slightly to the right in the direction of a clump of trees. At this point the path reappears. Tackle the flank of the mountain and make a rising traverse towards the left. Reach a cleft and ascend it to reach the south ridge, which is followed to the right to the summit.

Descent: Descend by the same route.

Route notes

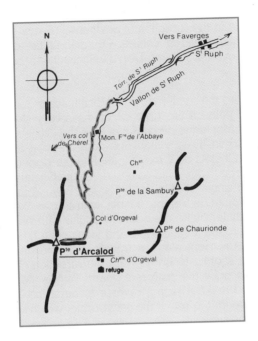

57 L'Arcalod

- height: 2,217 m
- starting point: Faverges, 26 km south of Annecy
- route: from the east
- grade: II
- climbing time: 4 hours 30 minutes
- views: very beautiful
- type of ground: woodland, grass, rocks

■ IGN map: 3432 OT– 1:25 000   Didier Richard No 2– 1:50 000
■ Chalet d'Orgeval Hut (private)   hut warden

Access: At Faverges, on the D12 southwards leading to the Col
de Tamié, go right in the direction of Seythenex (heavy goods
road) then right again towards Villaret and Glaise. Continue to
the end of the road, well beyond the hamlet of Saint-Ruph.
Beyond the asphalted section, the road is passable for motors for
a good distance (alt. 950 m).

Ascent: At the end of a broad track, cross the River Saint-Ruph
and climb up through the forest on a well marked and pleasant
path. Pass the house called Forestière de l'Abbaye (alt. 1,155 m).
At the exit from the forest, ignore a path on the right which
contours the Arcalod before joining the road to the Col de
Chérel. Pass a small forest shelter and, via a series of zig-zags,
reach the Col d'Orgeval (alt. 1,732 m). From the col the imposing
east face of the Arcalod is visible. This is the high point of the
route. Beyond the col and below it are the Chalets d'Orgeval. Do
not descend there but follow to the right a crest line which ends
up at a pole facing the east side of the Arcalod. When you are
level with this pole, turn right and, heading towards the face,
climb the steep grassy slope of an escarpment. Climb some
terraces to reach the wall in line with a big slab. From this point
onwards, care is essential. Get into a chimney-couloir which
splits the slab (easy, tricky section on rock to start with, good
holds). Then continue by a rising traverse to the left up a broad
cleft in the face, visible from the foot of the Arcalod. Reach level
ground just below the summit. Aim to the left to reach the narrow,
exposed crest and turn right to the top.

Descent: It is imperative to descend the same route. Do not
wander about. (Danger!)

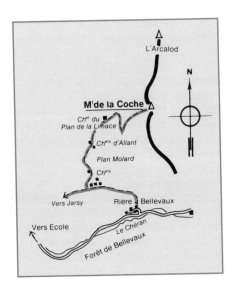

58 Mont de la Coche

- height: 2,070 m
- starting point: Ecole-en-Bauges (73), 35 km south of Annecy
- route: from the west
- grade: I
- climbing time: 3 hours 30 minutes
- views: beautiful
- type of ground: woodland, grass
- IGN map: 3432 OT – 1:25 000   Didier Richard No 2 – 1:50 000

Access: Either from Châtelard-en-Bauges or Saint-Pierre-d'Albigny and the Col du Frêne (N511), go to the village of Ecole-en-Bauges. Then take the Forêt de Bellevaux road which runs alongside the River Chéran. Ignore the little road on the right which climbs to the Notre-Dame-de-Bellevaux chapel and, about 1.5 km further on, take the broad track on the left which leads to the little hamlet of Rière-Bellevaux (alt. 989 m). Leave vehicles beside the houses (limited parking).

Ascent: Uphill from the hamlet, get on to the good path opposite the old school. Climb up first of all through a wood, then up a grassy slope. When you have gained some height, a long rocky barrier is visible on the right, dominating a big valley coming down from the crest directly in the line of ascent. Turn left and head towards the western end of this crest which one should follow eastwards as far as the Mont de la Coche, which is the continuation of the rocky barrier already mentioned. Reach a group of chalets on level land and work up a grassy slope to the right so as to reach the crest. Pass the Chalets d'Allant (alt. 1,580 m), then the Chalet du Plan de la Limace. Follow the line of the crest separating the Bellevaux pass from the western flank of the Arcalod. Go below a rocky point and reach a small col from where the small valley of Orgeval is visible. Climb the grassy slope to the right to the summit.

Descent: Descend by the same route.

Route notes

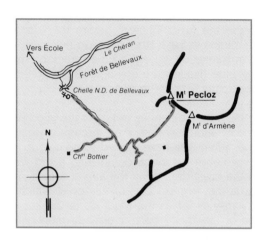

59   Le Pécloz

- height: 2,197 m
- starting point: Ecole-en-Bauges (73), 35 km south of Annecy
- route: from the west
- grade: I
- climbing time: 4 hours
- views: very beautiful
- type of ground: grass, stones
- IGN map: 3432 OT – 1:25 000   Didier Richard No 2 – 1:50 000

Access: From either Châtelard-en-Bauges or Saint-Pierre-d'Albigny and the Col du Frêne (N511), go to the village of Ecole-en-Bauges. Then take the Forêt de Bellevaux road which runs alongside the River Chéran and follow it for about 4 km before leaving it for a little road on the right, to reach the site of the ancient monastery of Bellevaux (alt. 907 m). Leave vehicles on the big platform at the end of the asphalted section of the road.

Ascent: Straight ahead, cross the River Nant de la Chapelle and turn left immediately to take the good path which runs alongside the stream and rises up a gentle slope through a pretty little valley. Pass close by the Notre-Dame-de-Bellevaux chapel. At the head of the valley, after a straight section, the path suddenly turns right to climb up through a forest. Leave it at this point and cross to the left the rough bed of a stream which is mostly dry. The tracks are practically non-existent here. On the other side of this rough area, after having climbed briefly along the bed of the stream, search on the left for a well marked path and ascend it. Higher up, ignore tracks on the right, which head towards the Montagne de la Lanche, and by a series of broad zig-zags reach a vast basin (alt. 1,650 m). The imposing rocky mass of Le Pécloz is easily regonizable to the left. Turning towards it, climb the long grassy slope in the valley between it and the Mont d'Armène. The tracks are not always very obvious. Reach the top of the valley, then turn off to the left, where good tracks are picked up again, and follow the line of the crest. Go round some big blocks, now on the left, now on the right and climb the steep terraces of the final slope.

Descent: Descend by the same route.

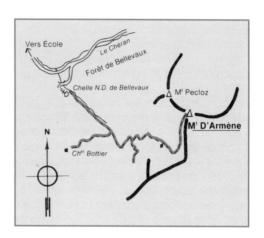

60   Mont d'Armène

- height: 2,158 m
- starting point: Ecole-en-Bauges (73), 35 km south of Annecy
- route: from the west
- grade: I
- climbing time: 3 hours
- views: very beautiful
- type of ground: grass
- IGN map: 3432 OT – 1:25 000   Didier Richard No 2 – 1:50 000

Access: From either Châtelard-en-Bauges or Saint-Pierre d'Albigny and the Col du Frêne, go to the village of Ecole-en-Bauges. Then take the Forêt de Bellevaux road, which runs alongside the River Chéran, for about 4 km before turning right on to a little road to the site of the ancient monastery of Bellevaux (alt. 907 m). Leave vehicles on the big platform at the end of the asphalted section of the road.

Ascent: Straight ahead, cross the Nant de la Chapelle stream and immediately turn left up the good path which runs alongside it, climbing gently up a pretty little valley. Pass close by the chapel of Notre-Dame-de-Bellevaux. At the head of the small valley, after a straight section, the path turns sharply right and climbs up through a forest. Leave it at this point and cross to the left over the rough area of a stream bed which is for the most part dry. Here the tracks are practically non-existent. On the other side of this rough ground, after having climbed briefly along the bed of the stream, look for a well marked path on the left and ascend it. Higher up, ignore the tracks on the right, which head towards the Montagne de la Lanche, and by a series of broad zig-zags reach a vast basin (alt. 1,650 m), dominated on the left by the imposing rocky mass of Le Pécloz, which is extended to the south-east by Mont d'Armène. Continue along the righthand edge of the basin (south-eastwards) on more or less obvious tracks. A little further on, the path bends to the right in the direction of a small col which separates the ridge rising to Mont d'Armène on the left from that of the Pointe des Arces on the right. Leave the path before the col and aim to the left to join the ridge of Mont d'Armène. Reach the summit via continuous zig-zags.

Descent: Descend by the same route.

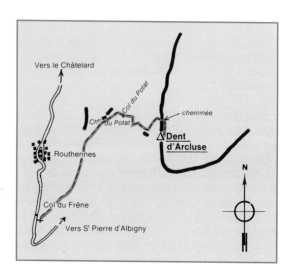

61 Dent d'Arcluse

- height: 2,040 m
- starting point: Saint-Pierre-d'Albigny (73), 27 km east of Chambéry
- route: from the west
- grade: II
- climbing time: 3 hours
- views: very beautiful
- type of ground: woodland, grass, rocks
- IGN map: 3432 OT–1:25 000   Didier Richard No 2–1:50 000

Access: From either Châtelard-en-Bauges or Saint-Pierre-d'Albigny to the Col du Frêne (alt. 950 m) where vehicles are left.

Ascent: Behind the cross on the col, take a well marked path which climbs a long wooded crest. Shortly after starting you come to an enormous meadow where the path disappears. It is thus necessary to locate the line of the crest and to work towards it. Some traces of the track are visible here and there. The path reappears clearly at the exit from the meadow, then remains well marked as one ascends the wooded section. On approaching the top of the crest, on a grassy flat area where a fence is crossed, turn slightly to the right and ignore the path which leads towards a long, narrow meadow. Now the wood gives way to a short grassy slope which leads to the Chalet du Potat, sited on the top of the crest. Via a short descent to the right of the chalet, reach the Col de Potat (alt. 1,351 m). Carry straight on and climb a steep, grassy slope (hard work) dominated by the rocky barrier on which stands the Dent d'Arcluse. On approaching the rocks, make a traverse to the left, then turn right towards the face. The path ascends a stony slope and arrives at a chimney which has to be climbed (good holds on the left). Emerge on to the narrow, rocky crest. Follow it to the right (some exposed sections) to reach the summit.

Descent: It is imperative to descend by the same route.

Route notes

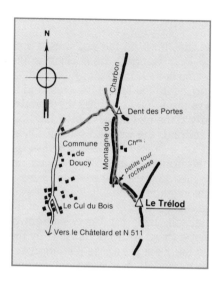

62 Le Trélod

- height: 2,181 m
- starting point: Doucy-en-Bauges (73), 35 km south of Annecy
- route: from the west
- grade: I
- climbing time: 3 hours 30 minutes
- views: very beautiful
- type of ground: woodland, grass, rocks
- IGN map: 3432 OT – 1:25 000   Didier Richard No 2 – 1:50 000

Access: From either Châtelard-en-Bauges or Saint-Pierre d'Albigny and the Col du Frène (N533), go to the village of Doucy-en-Bauges via La Compôte. Continue beyond Doucy as far as the end of the D60, level with a wood. Space for a few vehicles (alt. 1,200 m).

Ascent: Do not take the track straight ahead but enter an enclosure on the right and ascend the grassy slope. Halfway up, leave it on the left and cross a barrier. The path is not easy to find, for at this point it is very furrowed and in part concealed by undergrowth. However, you can pick it up on the right outside the enclosure as it rises in zig-zags through a dense wood to arrive at the rocky base of the Montagne du Charbon. Climb this rocky section on good tracks and emerge on to the grassy crest. Aim to the right and follow the crest as far as the point where it drops slightly (chalets below to the left). On the left the imposing mass of Le Trélod dominates the continuation of the crest. Continue southwards. The path is poorly marked for a few metres on approaching a small rocky tower on the crest. Go round this on the left. At this point, abandon the tracks which continue southwards and aim boldly to the left, towards the long grassy ridge which rises towards the summit. Climb it on the well marked path to reach the rocky blocks of the summit section and the signal marking the peak.

Descent: Descend by the same route.

Route notes

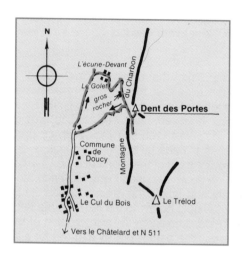

63 Dent des Portes

- **height:** 1,932 m
- **starting point:** Doucy-en-Bauges (73), 35 km south of Annecy
- **route:** from the west
- **grade:** I
- **climbing time:** 2 hours 30 minutes
- **views:** beautiful
- **type of ground:** grass
- **IGN map:** 3432 OT– 1:25 000   Didier Richard No 2– 1:50 000

Access: From either Châtelard-en-Bauges or Saint-Pierre-d'Albigny and the Col du Frêne (N511) go to the village of Doucy-en-Bauges via La Compôte. Continue beyond Doucy to the end of the D60, level with a wood. Space here for a few vehicles (alt. 1,200 m).

Ascent: Take the broad track straight ahead which climbs a gentle slope to the Chalets du Gollet and de l'Ecurie-Devant (alt. 1,380 m). Take the path on the side of a sort of big cement basin which rises in the direction of the rocky barrier to the east and leads towards a clump of trees. The poorly marked path is not easy to follow as it crosses numerous rivulets on both sides. Halfway up the slope, between the chalets and the rocky barrier, aim sharply to the right in the direction of a big rock and make a rising traverse to the base of the barrier. Once up against the wall, climb it by going up the fault on good tracks. Emerge on to the crest and ignore the path on the right which leads towards Le Trélod. Turn left and quickly reach the nearby summit via an easy slope.

Descent: Descend by the same route. It is possible to rejoin one's vehicle by a fairly steep path which goes straight down the slope, starting from the point where one leaves the wall.

Route notes

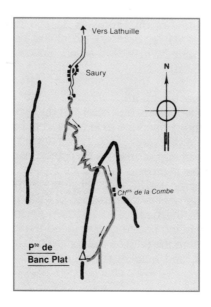

64 Pointe de Banc Plat

- height: 1,907 m
- starting point: Lathuille, 19 km south of Annecy
- route: from the north
- grade: I
- climbing time: 3 hours
- views: beautiful
- type of ground: woodland, grass, rocks
- IGN map: 3431 OT– 1:25 000   Didier Richard No 2– 1:50 000

Access: From Annecy take the N508 as far as Bout-du-Lac and then the D180 to the village of Lathuille. Right of the church, take the small road which leads to Saury. Carry on as far as the end of the asphalted road, where there is parking for vehicles (alt. 700 m).

Ascent: At the end of the car park, take a stony path on the right and just afterwards, level with a chalet, a second path on the left. After a grassy slope, start to climb up through the forest, then suddenly take another path well to the left. Continue through the forest and, after a long series of zig-zags, arrive at a rocky barrier and cross its flank. Emerge into a vale half forest, half copse, and at the end of this wooded section reach the mountain pasture Chalets de la Combe (alt. 1,572 m). From the chalets, the Pointe de Banc Plat is visible on the continuation of the rocky barrier on the right. Continue up the small valley and cross a short rocky section on a staircase which allows one to reach the crest. Where the path bends to the right, leave it to take the tracks more to the right which enable you to climb a grassy shoulder and reach a basin. Traverse this basin in the direction of the rocky barrier, cross a fence and reach the summit via some zig-zags.

Descent: Descend by the same route.

Route notes

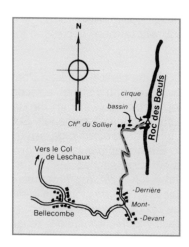

65   Roc des Boeufs

- height: 1,774 m
- starting point: Bellecombe-en-Bauges (73), 24 km south of Annecy
- route: from the west
- grade: II
- climbing time: 3 hours
- views: beautiful
- type of ground: grass, stones, rocks
- IGN map: 3431 OT– 1:25 000   Didier Richard No 2– 1:50 000

Access: From Annecy on the N508 to Sévrier, the N512 to the Col de Leschaux, then the D10 and D61 to Bellecombe-en-Bauges. In the village take a little road on the left which leads to the hamlet of Mont (about 2 km), which is divided into two groups of houses: Mont-Devant au Sud and Mont-Derrière au Nord. Make for the latter and leave vehicles at the end of the road, level with the last houses (alt. 1,050 m).

Ascent: Follow the good track which continues the road north-wards to reach in under an hour the Chalets du Sollier (alt. 1,450 m) from where the view drops down towards the Col de Leschaux. The long rocky barrier of the Roc des Boeufs dominates the countryside to the east. To the right of the chalets, head towards a pond and stop there, so as to locate the precise point at which to climb this long face. Contrary to what one would think, this point is not the summit of this rock situated a little to the right on the crest and topped with a cross. It is in fact a more modest block to the left of this point and also provided with a cross. From the pond, facing the rocky barrier, a boulder field can be seen higher up. Start up the grassy slope and contour to the right around a wood of fir trees. Having arrived at the boulder field, climb to the top to arrive at the face in a sort of small cirque. At the top on the left, climb an easy chimney and emerge on the right on to flat ground, near the crest. Near the big rock, climb another easy chimney to the left, then climb the summit block on the right by a fairly easy crack.

Descent: Descend by the same route and, above all, do not wander about between the summit and the boulder field.

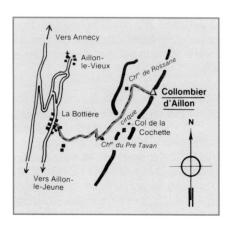

66 Colombier d'Aillon

- height: 2,043 m
- starting point: Aillon-le-Vieux (73), 25 km south of Annecy
- route: from the west
- grade : I
- climbing time : 3 hours
- views: very beautiful
- type of ground: woodland, grass
- IGN map: 3432 OT– 1:25 000   Didier Richard No 2– 1:50 000

Access: From Annecy on the D5 to the village of Lescheraines (8 km before Le Châtelard-en-Bauges). From there take the D59 which leads to Aillon-le-Jeune. Follow it for about 8 km, then turn left in the direction of Aillon-le-Vieux and right 1 km further on to join the D206 at the hamlet of La Bottière where vehicles can be left (alt. 920 m).

Ascent: If arriving from the direction of Aillon-le-Vieux, immediately take a road suitable for motors on the left between some houses and follow it about a hundred metres. Now leave it and, immediately after a spring, take a well marked path on the left. Follow this briefly, then when it veers to the left, take another path which goes off to the right. Go up towards the mountain and arrive at a narrow grassy valley. There the path disappears and one needs to climb this valley entirely without bothering about tracks which start on the right. Up above, the path reappears at the entrance to a wood. Ascend the wooded slope and emerge into a clearing at the Chalet de Pré-Tavan. Turn left and traverse a wood, then via the right and a short stony slope, reach a cirque dominated by the Colombier d'Aillon. Aim to the left and go as far as the Chalet de Rossane (alt. 1,738 m) which is visible on stepping into the cirque. Practically at the level of the chalet, move to the right up the final steep grassy slope (laborious) to reach the fairly exposed summit.

Descent: Descend by the same route.

Route notes

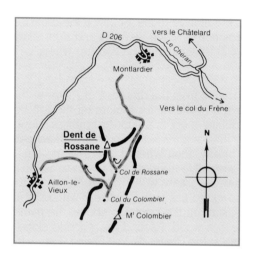

67   Dent de Rossane

- height: 1,891 m
- starting point: Le Châtelard-en-Bauges (73), 30 km south of Annecy
- route: from the north
- grade: I
- climbing time: 3 hours
- views: beautiful
- type of ground: woodland, grass
- IGN map: 3432 OT – 1:25 000   Didier Richard No 2 – 1:50 000

Access: From Annecy via the Col de Leschaux (N512) to Le Châtelard-en-Bauges. Continue in the direction of the Col du Frêne for about 1 km, as far as the bridge at Escorchevel which crosses the River Chéran. Turn right on to the D206 in the direction of Aillon-le-Vieux, then about 2 km further on turn left to reach the hamlet of Montlardier. Leave vehicles at the top of the small village, near the last houses (alt. 750 m).

Ascent: Ascend a good path by the side of the spring. Quickly reach the dense forest where the path winds up a very steep slope, sometimes painfully so. At the exit from the forest, one arrives at the Combe de l'Ilette (alt. 1,550 m). Ascend this in a straight line as far as the Col de Rossane (alt. 1,782 m). Now leave the path, which continues straight on in the direction of the Col du Colombier, and turn sharply to the right to reach the summit easily.

Descent: Descend by the same route or go as far as the basin situated between the Col de Rossane and the Col du Colombier. Then, if you have arranged transport back from Montlardier or Aillon-le-Vieux, aiming to the right, descend into a big valley following a more or less well marked path on the righthand side, which leads to Aillon-le-Vieux (5 km from Montlardier).

Route notes

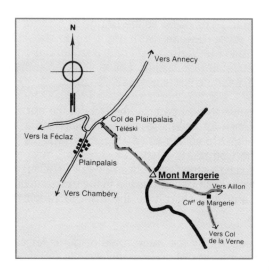

68   Mont Margerie

- height: 1,845 m
- starting point: Les Déserts-Plainpalais (73), 17 km north-east of Chambéry
- route: from the north-west
- grade: II
- climbing time: 2 hours 30 minutes
- views: very beautiful
- type of ground: woodland, stony, rocks
- IGN map: 3432 OT – 1:25 000   Didier Richard No 2 – 1:50 000

Access: From Chambéry via the N512 and Les Déserts to the Col de Plainpalais. Turn right at the col and drive towards the small ski lift station. Leave vehicles on the car park at the end of the motor road (alt. 1,170 m).

Ascent: Climb the stony slope alongside the ski lift cable as far as the last pylon. Continue to the right on a well marked path which climbs up through the forest. At the exit from the wooded section, ascend a boulder field leading towards the rocky base of the mountain. Be careful not to go round left in line with a rocky tooth. Reach the foot of the final rise. Climb the very steep and exposed rocks (iron rails and ladders) and emerge at an easily accessible chimney. Climb to the intersection of several chimney-couloirs which criss-cross the summit block. Use the couloir facing you and ascend it as far as the Trou de l'Agneau (sign, arrow). Thus quickly to the summit on the right.

Descent: Descend by the same route. It is equally possible to descend from the summit on the eastern side towards Aillon-le-Jeune. The path passes the Chalet de Margerie and the Forêt de Margerie to reach the D59 in the vicinity of Rocquerand (quite near to Aillon-le-Jeune). In this case, leave a vehicle here for the rego round.

Route notes

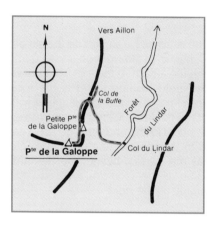

69 Pointe de la Galoppe

- height: 1,680 m
- starting point: Aillon-le-Jeune (73), 37 km south of Annecy
- route: from the east
- grade: I
- climbing time: 2 hours 30 minutes
- views: very beautiful
- type of ground: woodland, grass
- IGN map: 3432 OT– 1:25 000   Didier Richard No 2– 1:50 000

Access: From Annecy on the N512 via the Col de Leschaux and Lescheraines where one takes the D59 to the village of Aillon-le-Jeune. Just before the church, turn off left in the direction of the station and a little further on, at the junction which leads to the ski lift, continue on the right as far as the Col du Lindar where vehicles can be left (alt. 1,190 m).

Ascent: At the col, take a path on the right which enters the forest and descends to the bottom of a ravine. Cross a small stream and go up the opposite side of the ravine. Continue to climb the wooded slope and, aiming to the right, reach the Col de la Buffe (alt. 1,439 m). On the crest, follow another path to the left to a small watering hole. Carry on southwards and further on go round the Petite Pointe de la Galoppe on its western flank (beware, short tricky section), finally emerging into a little basin. Ascend the easy grassy slope as far as the crest and go to the summit to the right.

Descent: Descend by the same route.

Route notes

6. BEAUFORTAIN

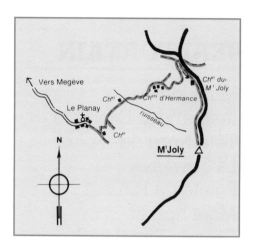

70 | Mont Joly

- height: 2,525 m
- starting point: Megève
- route: from the west
- grade: I
- climbing time: 3 hours
- views: magnificent
- type of ground: grass
- IGN map: 3531 OT – 1:25 000   Didier Richard No 8 – 1:50 000

Access: In the centre of Megève, take the road to Mont d'Arbois and follow it as far as Planellet (4 km). Ignore the road on the right signposted to Altiport-Côte 2000 and continue straight on to the end of the motor road at the hamlet of Planay. Spaces to leave vehicles (alt. 1,450 m).

Ascent: Take the broad path straight ahead and a little further on, in sight of a chalet on the open slope to the left, take another path in this direction. A little higher up, pay no attention to a path which starts on the right. Head northwards, passing in front of an imposing chalet, cross a small stream then, after a series of zig-zags through undergrowth and a grassy slope, reach the Chalets d'Hermance (alt. 1,827 m). Continue beyond them as far as the crest where one ignores the path on the left heading towards Mont Joux, and the one which descends the opposite side of the crest to Saint-Nicolas-de-Véroce. Follow the crest to the right to the Chalet du Mont Joly. Head due south following the line of the crest all the time and after some fairly steep sections emerge on to the summit, with its view indicator.

Descent: Descend by the same route

Route notes

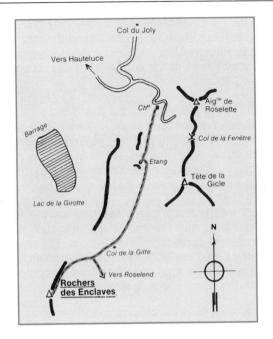

71   Rochers des Enclaves

- height: 2,465 m
- starting point: Hauteluce (73), 24 km north-east of Albertville
- route: from the north-east
- grade: I
- climbing time: 2 hours 30 minutes
- views: magnificent
- type of ground: grass, stones
- IGN map: 3531 OT – 1:25 000   Didier Richard No 8 – 1:50 000

Access: From Albertville, go to the village of Hauteluce via the N525, leading to Beaufort, and the D218. Continue in the direction of the Col du Joly for about 10 km, i.e. as far as the col. Now turn off right at a hairpin bend on to a good motor road signposted to the Col de la Fenêtre. Stop level with the last mountain farmhouse on the right where vehicles can be left (alt. 1,975 m).

Ascent: Behind the farm, take a path which rises southwards along a sort of promontory. Reach a small lake at the foot of a cliff. Climb to the left up a series of zig-zags and, via a long easy slope, emerge on to the Col de la Gitte (alt. 2,359 m). The col is very broad and the view unobstructed all around. Aim to the right and follow the line of the crest. Via a gentle slope, head towards the long natural barrier which makes up the Rochers des Enclaves, topped by a signal visible from afar. You can reach the summit easily. On the southern side of the summit may be found crystals and numerous crystalline stones. Given its simplicity, this ascent can be made with children.

Descent: Descend by the same route.

Route notes

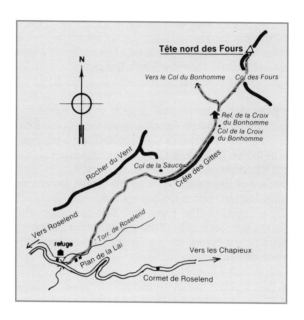

72 Tête Nord des Fours

- height: 2,756 m
- starting point: Beaufort (73), 20 km east of Albertville
- route: from the south-west
- grade: I
- climbing time: 4 hours
- views: magnificent
- type of ground: grass, stones
- IGN map: 3531 OT – 1:25 000   Didier Richard No 8 – 1:50 000

- ■ Plan de la Lai Hut (CAF)
  hut warden   Tel: 79 89 67 78
- ■ Croix du Bonhomme Hut (CAF)
  hut warden   Tel: 79 07 05 28

Access: From Albertville on the N525 to Beaufort, then from there
to the Lac de Roselend. Go around the lake on the left and climb
in the direction of the Cormet de Roselend. Immediately after
crossing a gorge, the road reaches Plan de la Lai (alt. 1,800 m), a
big platform before the last sharp bends leading to the Cormet
de Roselend. Leave vehicles on this platform, near a small bridge
(about 4 km from the lake).

Ascent: Just after the bridge, take a track on the left with the sign
'GR5' (Hiking Path No.5). Ascend the enormous pastures following the red and white painted way marks. Pass the Chalets de
Chavannes then, aiming slightly to the right, emerge at the Col de
la Sauce. Ignore a path on the left which descends to La Gitte and
continue to the right along the GR5 which goes along the Crête
des Gittes. The panoramic path includes some sections which are
a little exposed but not difficult. The end of the crest drops easily
to end at the Col de la Croix du Bonhomme (alt. 2,443 m). Ascend
behind the Touring-Club de France hut and briefly follow the
path to the Col du Bonhomme, then leave it to turn right in the
direction of a high tension pylon. Pass the base of this and
continue to the Col des Fours (alt. 2,673 m). Ignoring the Tête Sud
des Fours on the right of the col, continue to the left and ascend a
schist slope leading to the Tête Nord, provided with a view
indicator.

Descent: Descend by the same route. It is possible to descend
directly to the Cormet de Roselend from the Col de la Croix du
Bonhomme by following tracks below the Crête des Gittes on its
southern side.

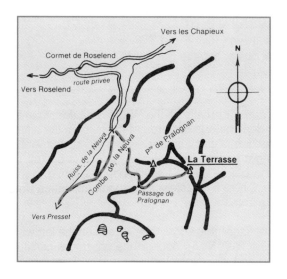

73　La Terrasse

- height: 2,893 m
- starting point: Beaufort (73), 20 km east of Albertville
- route: from the west
- grade: II
- climbing time: 3 hours 30 minutes
- views: very beautiful
- type of ground: grass, stones, rocks
- IGN map: 3531 OT– 1:25 000　　Didier Richard No 8– 1:50 000
- Plan de la Lai Hut (CAF)
  hut warden　Tel: 79 89 07 78

Access: From Albertville via the N525 and Beaufort to the Lac de Roselend. Go around the lake on the left and ascend as far as Cormet de Roselend (alt. 1,968 m) where there is a car park.

Ascent: To the right of the car park, take a private motor road forbidden to other vehicles. This enters the Combe de la Neuva and goes to a small reservoir belonging to the E.D.F. (Electricité de France). At this spot, cross left over the Nueva stream and make a rising traverse to the left in the direction of the slope opposite. Do not trust some existing tracks which could throw you off route. The slope towards which one should be making comprises a variety of cirques. Go towards the second starting from the bottom of the valley, separated from the first by the Pointe de Pralognan (alt. 2,665 m), the western ridge of which plunges into the valley. First of all, ascend a steep but short grassy slope, then a less steep boulder field and make for the head of the cirque, towards the left. Then take the tracks which climb the face and emerge on to the crest between two cairns at the Passage de Pralognan. La Terrasse, topped by a rocky rise, is to the left and a large cairn is visible on its summit. Descend slightly into a big basin, keeping to the left, and head for a boulder field situated between the summit of La Terrasse and a secondary rocky rise on the left. Ascend the steep boulder field to a gap, turn right and reach the summit up easy rocks.

Descent: Descend by the same route.

Route notes

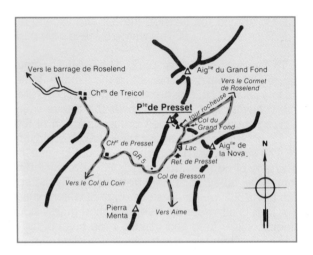

74   Pointe de Presset

- height: 2,759 m
- starting point: Beaufort (73), 20 km east of Albertville
- route: from the south
- grade: I
- climbing time: 4 hours
- views: very beautiful
- type of ground: grass, stones
- equipment necessary: ice axe
- IGN map: 3532 OT – 1:25 000   Didier Richard No 8 – 1:50 000
- Presset Hut (CAF)
  no warden

Access: From Albertville to Beaufort on the N525, then from there to the Lac de Roselend. Go along the righthand side of the lake and cross the dam, then ascend in the direction of the Col du Pré. At a hairpin bend, take a road suitable for motors on the left, signposted to Treicol. Follow the road, which overlooks the lake, to its end, i.e. the Chalets de Treicol. However, one is recommended to leave vehicles just before the chalets, near a track which heads towards the other shore of the lake (alt. 1,700 m).

Ascent: From the Chalets de Treicol, ascend the small valley southwards, following the GR5 (Hiking Path No.5) way-marked in red and white. Via a gentle slope reach the Chalet de Presset (alt. 2,011 m) situated on a big platform. Ignore the path which heads towards the Col du Coin, which can be seen to the southwest, and turn left (still on GR5). Climb a slightly steeper slope in the direction of the long rocky barrier to the east, headed on the extreme left by the Aiguille du Grand Fond, in front of which is the Pointe de Presset. In the vicinity of the Col de Bresson (alt. 2,473 m) the view of the monolithic Pierra Menta (to the right) is striking. Cross the col and leave the GR5, then traverse the eastern slope leftwards to reach in 15 minutes the Presset Hut, owned by the CAF (alt. 2,505 m). From this point, looking northeastwards (i.e. behind the hut), one can make out not far off two cols separated from each other by a big rock island. Head in the direction of the lefthand of these (Col du Grand Fond), overshadowed by the Pointe de Presset. Pass near the little Lac de Presset, nestling in a hollow near the hut, and after a short, fairly steep slope, emerge on to the col (alt. 2,676 m). To the left of the col, go round a rocky tower on the right and ascend a small, fairly steep couloir often covered with snow (care required, ice axe sometimes useful). Finally go to the right up the ridge to the summit.

Descent: Descend by the same route.

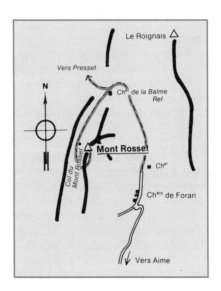

75 Mont Rosset

- height: 2,446 m
- starting point: Aime (73), 14 km north-east of Moûtiers
- route: from the north
- grade: I
- climbing time: 2 hours 30 minutes
- views: very beautiful
- type of ground: grass, stones
- IGN map: 3532 OT– 1:25 000   Didier Richard No 8– 1:50 000
- Balme Hut (community property)
  hut warden

Access: From Albertville take the N90 in the direction of Bourg-Saint-Maurice to reach the small town of Aime. To the right of the church, take the D86, pass the Côte-d'Aime, then ignore the Granier road on the left. A little higher up, before Valezan, turn left on to the road signposted to the Pont de la Gitte and follow it to its end by the Chalets de Foran (alt. 1,650 m).

Ascent: Just before the Chalets de Foran, take no notice of a track on the left signposted to Mont Rosset; this is not the route to use. Continue straight ahead on the broad path (GR5) signposted to Grand Fond-Presset and ascend a small, slightly inclined, valley northwards. At the head of the valley, the path turns left (west) and leads rapidly to the Chalet de la Balme Hut (alt. 2,009 m). Now abandon the GR5, which continues northwards towards Presset. Aim to the left and head southwards, contouring around Mont Rosset. Ascend a valley and reach the Col du Mont Rosset (alt. 2,333 m). At this point it is tempting to go straight for the summit by way of the ridge on the left. Continue to traverse to the left without losing height, on the western flank of the mountain, and emerge on to the crest a little below and to the right of the summit. Turn left to reach the peak.

Descent: Descend by the same route

Route notes

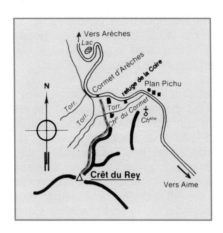

76 Crêt du Rey - North side

- height: 2,639 m
- starting point: Arêches (73), 25 km east of Albertville; Aime (73), 14 km north-east of Moûtiers
- route: from the north-east
- grade: I
- climbing time: 2 hours
- views: very beautiful
- type of ground: grass, stones
- IGN map: 3532 OT – 1:25 000   Didier Richard No 8 – 1:50 000
- Coire Hut (community property)
  hut warden   Tel: 79 09 70 92 (town hall)

Access: Two possibilities:

1) *Beaufortain side*. At Albertville, take the N525 as far as Beaufort and the D218 to Arêches. About 1 km above Arêches, in the direction of the Col du Pré, take the road on the right (still the D218) which leads to the dam at Saint-Guérin. At the dam, turn left and, a little higher up, take a metalled road on the right which overlooks the lake and leads to the Cormet d'Arêches.

2) *Tarentaise side*. At Aime, between Moûtiers and Bourg-Saint-Maurice, take the D218 (well maintained mountain road) which leads directly to the Cormet d'Arêches. Leave vehicles on the platform at the col (alt. 2,107 m).

Ascent: The Crêt du Rey lies to the south of the Cormet d'Arêches at the end of a long ridge. It is easily located by the trig point on its summit. From the col (coming from the direction of Arêches), follow tracks on the right (southwards) which ascend a slightly inclined grassy slope, bordered on the left by a very low rocky crest (only 45 metres above the height of the col). Not far ahead (about 10 minutes) the Chalets du Cormet are visible below on the left. At this point the tracks are rather confused and it is better not to bother with them. Level with the chalets, climb a steep grassy slope to the right giving access to the top of the crest mentioned above. Follow this as far as the level ground in front of the summit. The section which follows, steep and stony, appears forbidding but is, nevertheless, easily tackled.

Descent: Descend by the same route.

Route notes

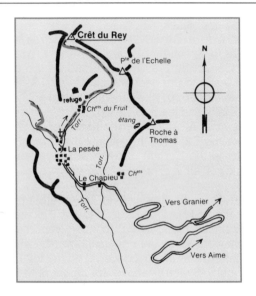

77 Crêt du Rey - South side

- height: 2,639 m
- starting point: Tessens (73), 17 km north-east of Moûtiers
- route: from the south
- grade: I
- climbing time: 3 hours
- views: very beautiful
- type of ground: grass, stones
- IGN map: 3532 OT – 1:25 000   Didier Richard No 8 – 1:50 000
- Plagne Hut (community property)
  Tel: 79 55 69 46 (town hall)

Access: From Albertville, on the N90 which leads to Bourg-Saint-Maurice, to the small town of Aime. Left of the church, take the D218 to Tessens. Continue in the direction of Granier and take the second road on the left after leaving Tessens (signpost to La Pesée). Follow the little asphalted road as far as the Chalets du Chapieu (alt. 1,691 m). A road suitable for motors continues to Pesée. However, it is recommended that vehicles be left by the bridge crossing the River Nant de Tessens, only a few hundred metres after Le Chapieu, not far from La Pesée (alt. 1,700 m).

Ascent: Continue along the road through the fairly large group of houses spread out on the slope at La Pesée. Climb up as far as the last chalet and, leaving the track which leads northwards, ascend to the right up a steep grassy slope practically devoid of tracks in the direction of a white cross nearby. Pass the cross and, aiming to the right, join a track which is followed more or less as far as the Chalets du Fruit. Keep going in the same direction (north-eastwards) and pass the last chalet. Keep straight on and go right up the gentle slope of a broad valley. High up, aim to the left to get to a vast cirque, dominated at its head by the Crêt du Rey, recognizable by the trig point on its summit. Head for the top of the cirque (north-westwards) following the base of the crest on your right. Right at the end, climb to the crest at its lowest point and go round right to reach the summit.

Descent: Descend by the same route.

Route notes

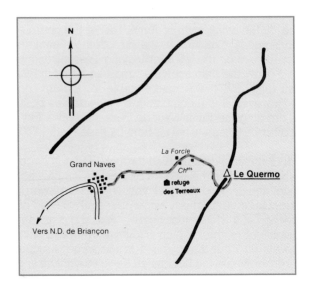

78   Le Quermo

- height: 2,301 m
- starting point: Notre-Dame-de Briancon (hamlet of Grand-Naves), 31 km south-east of Albertville
- route: from the west
- grade: I
- climbing time: 3 hours
- views: magnificent
- type of ground: grass, stones
- IGB map: 3532 West
- Terreaux Hut (community property)
  no warden Tel: 79 24 01 73 (town hall)

Access: At Albertville, take the N90 as far as Notre-Dame-de-Briancon, then at the end of the village take the D93 on the left as far as Grand-Naves. Leave vehicles on a proper car park by the last of the houses (alt. 1,340 m).

Ascent: Le Quermo lies due east of Grand-Naves on the long crest which blocks the horizon. Climb up above the car park along a very steep village alley way. After the last house, follow a good path north-eastwards which leads to a nearby chalet. The tracks now incline more to the east to reach the Chalets de la Forcle via a gentle slope. Climb a short and slightly steeper slope on the right to the last chalet. From here, the summit is seen clearly ahead (to the east). Go straight up it. When the slope becomes really steep, head right and, by a rising traverse, reach the crest at a level bit of ground, well below and to the right of the summit. Now head northwards along the crest to the final peak topped by a signal tower.

Descent: Descend by the same route.

Route notes

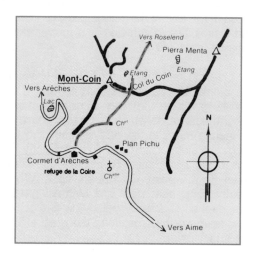

79   Mont Coin

- height: 2,541 m
- starting point: Arêches (73), 25 km east of Albertville; Aime (73), 14 km north-east of Moûtiers
- route: from the south
- grade: I
- climbing time: 1 hour 30 minutes
- views: very beautiful
- type of ground: grass
- IGN map: 3532 OT– 1:25 000   Didier Richard No 8– 1:50 000
- Coire Hut (community property)
  hut warden   Tel: 79 09 73 59 (town hall)

Access: Two possibilities:
1) *Beaufortain side.* At Albertville, take the N525 as far as Beaufort and the D218 to Arêches. About 1 km above Arêches, in the direction of the Col du Pré, take the road on the right (still the D218) which leads to the dam at Saint-Guérin. At the dam, turn left and a little higher up take a metalled road which overlooks the lake and leads to the Cormet d'Arêches.
2) *Tarentaise side.* At Aime, between Moûtiers and Bourg-Saint-Maurice, take the D218 (well maintained mountain road) which leads directly to the Cormet d'Arêches. Leave vehicles on the platform at the col (alt. 2,107 m).

Ascent: From the Cormet d'Arêches, follow briefly the road which descends on the Tarentaise side and then take the first track you find on the left, slightly below the col. Follow it as far as a fairly imposing mountain chalet and, turning northwards, head towards the Col du Coin which splits the long crest running east-west. Climb an easy grassy slope on good tracks to reach the col (alt. 2,409 m). Follow the crest to the left as far as the foot of a rise which you need to go round on the right. Ascend the next small boulder field which enables one to rejoin the crest at a sort of gap. Finally cross the fairly steep summit rock (exposed and tricky section) to reach the peak.

Descent: Descend by the same route.

Route notes

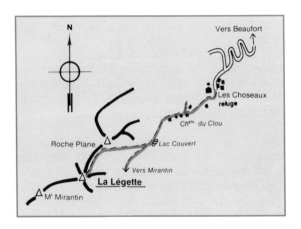

80 La Légette du Mirantin

- height: 2,356 m
- starting point: Beaufort (73), 20 km east of Albertville
- route: from the north-east
- grade: I
- climbing time: 3 hours 30 minutes
- views: very beautiful
- type of ground: grass, stones
- IGN map: 3532 OT– 1:25 000   Didier Richard No 8– 1:50 000

Access: From Albertville on the N525 to Beaufort. Go right in the direction of Arêches, then immediately turn again to the right. Cross the bridge and turn left by the Ponts et Chaussées (Highways Department) building to follow the small road which goes to the hamlet of Les Choseaux. Continue to the end of the road where there are spaces for parking cars (alt. 1,300 m).

Ascent: Take the path straight ahead and make for a farm situated uphill on the right. Above this, ascend a grassy slope, go through a wood and then continue across pastures. Pass several mountain chalets and reach the last group, the Chalets du Clou. Clamber up and aim to the left (southwards) in the direction of some fir trees. Cross a short wooded section and, on good tracks up a grassy slope, reach the Lac Couvert, a sort of pond almost full of plants, lying in a hollow. La Légette is visible beyond the lake to the south-west. Further to the right one can make out the summit of the Roche Plane. The two summits are joined by a grassy crest which dips to form a sort of col. Immediately after passing the lake, leave the path, which carries on further southwards, and turn right to face the Roche Plane. Ascend the zigzags on practically non-existent tracks. Further on the tracks become more obvious. Follow them to reach the crest at its lowest point. Continue southwards along the now sharply steepening but fairly easy crest (some sections amongst blocks of rock) as far as the base of the rocky summit block. Between the almost vertical rocks and a barrier on the left, ascend a scree couloir and above move to the right to the summit.

Descent: Descend by the same route.

81   Mont Mirantin

- height: 2,461 m
- starting point: Arêches (73), 25 km east of Albertville
- route: from the south-east
- grade: II
- climbing time: 3 hours 30 minutes
- views: very beautiful
- type of ground: grass, stones
- equipment necessary: rope
- IGN map: 3532 OT – 1:25 000   Didier Richard No 8 – 1:50 000

Access: At Albertville, take the N525 to Beaufort, then the D218 to Arêches and the D65 as far as the small village of La Dray at the end of the road, about 4 km south of Arêches. Parking for vehicles by the side of the chapel (alt. 1,200 m).

Ascent: Opposite the chapel and uphill from the village, take the path which runs alongside the meadow fences and ascend a grassy valley bordered on each side by a wood. Reach the top of the valley (about 30 min) and emerge on to a platform at the Chalets de Plan-Villard. Turn left along a crest and ascend a grassy slope which follows. Bending to the left the path suddenly emerges on to the southern slope. Below, the Chalet de Mirantin is visible. Do not go to this chalet, but instead traverse right on the flank of the mountain (red way marks) and soon reach the Chalet du Lac, situated on a flat area above the Chalet de Mirantin (water point). Continue traversing, keeping always to the right, and heading for the long crest blocking the horizon. Ascend an easy boulder field (red way-marks) and reach the top at a pronounced subsidence in the crest. The summit of Mont Mirantin lies to the right at the end of the ridge and has a signal point which enables it to be identified correctly. Walk to the right along the narrow ridge, cross some easy rocky sections, as well as a gap (tricky), and reach the culminating point. It takes about 20 minutes to climb this ridge.

Descent: Descend by the same route.

Route notes

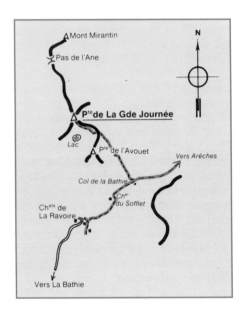

82 Pointe de la Grande Journée

- height: 2,462 m
- starting point: La Bâthie (73), 7 km south-east of Albertville
- route: from the south
- grade: I
- climbing time: 4 hours
- views: very beautiful
- type of ground: grass, stones
- IGN map: 3532 OT – 1:25 000   Didier Richard No 8 – 1:50 000

Access: At Albertville, take the N90 in the direction of Moûtiers. Leave it about 7 km further on where you turn to the left to get to the village of La Bâthie. At the top of the village, take a very steep little road on the left (D65) and climb to a height of about 1,350 metres. Firstly one passes several small hamlets, including Brun and Le Fugier, with signs indicating their altitude. At a bend, take a little metalled motor road on the right to get to the Chalets de la Ravoire (alt. 1,350 m). Leave vehicles near the bridge, just before the last bend in the road.

Ascent: At this last bend, take a good track on the right and leave it almost immediately to turn left on to a path which rises north-eastwards, at first through a small wood, then over enormous pastures. Level with the Chalet du Sofflet, the only building one comes to, cross the stream to the left and pass the front of the building. Continue north-eastwards all the time and reach the Col de la Bâthie (alt. 1,892 m), dominated on the left by the Pointe de Lavouet. From this point on, the route is not very obvious and it is essential to follow the numerous red way marks which mark the route as far as the crest. From the Col de la Bâthie, turn left and follow the line of a crest which contours the Pointe de Lavouet on the right. In the vicinity of a big valley, which is to be avoided, aim to the left and reach the crest situated between the Pointe de Lavouet (on the left) and the Pointe de la Grande Journée (on the right). Now turn right and follow this crest to the peak.

Descent: Descend by the same route

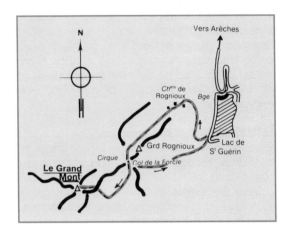

83 Le Grand Mont

- height: 2,687 m
- starting point: Arêches (73), 25 km east of
  Albertville
- route: from the north-east
- grade: I
- climbing time: 3 hours 30 minutes
- views: magnificent
- type of ground: woodland, grass, stones
- IGN map: 3532 OT– 1:25 000   Didier Richard No 8– 1:50 000
- Chalet des Gravettes Hut (private)
  hut warden   Tel: 79 38 14 51

Access: From Albertville to Arêches via the N525 to Beaufort and
the D218. About 1 km above Arêches, in the direction of the Col
du Pré, take the road on the right (still the D218) which leads to
the dam at Saint-Guérin. Cross the dam and follow the motor road
on the west shore of Lac Saint-Guérin. Leave vehicles at the end
of the lake, level with a signpost to Le Grand Mont (alt. 1,560 m).

Ascent: Take the path on the right to Le Grand Mont which rises
northwards through woodland. At the end of the wooded section,
reach the first mountain chalet, then two more (Chalets de Rognioux). Head towards the south-west, sighting on a big rocky
tooth (Grand Rognioux). Pass its foot and ascend a big easy
corridor which reaches the Col de la Forcle (alt. 2,378 m). To the
right of the col is the vast cirque of the northern slope of Le Grand
Mont. Cross the col and traverse south-westwards, below a long
rocky crest. Aim to the right and climb a fairly steep but easy
couloir which gives access to the crest. Turn left and reach the
nearby summit.

Descent: Descend by the same route. It is possible to descend
more directly to the lake. For that, just before the Col de la
Forcle, turn right and descend the steep slope running
eastwards.

Route notes

7. ■ VANOISE-TARENTAISE

84. La Grande Lanche
85. Le Grand Arc
86. Mont Bellachat
87. Pointe de Combe Bronsin
88. Pic du Rognolet
89. Grand Pic de la Lauzière
90. Le Gros Villan
91. Le Cheval Noir
92. Mont Jovet
93. Mont du Borgne
94. Le Breguin (or Brequin)
95. Petit Mont-Blanc
96. Pointe de la Réchasse
97. Pointe des Pichères
98. Pointe de Friolin
99. Aiguille Grive
100. Tête du Ruitor

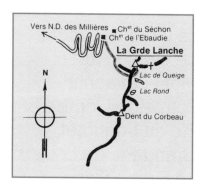

84 La Grande Lanche

- height: 2,110 m
- starting point: Notre-Dame-des-Millières (73), 5 km south of Albertville
- route: from the west
- grade: I
- climbing time: 2 hours
- views: very beautiful
- type of ground: grass, stones
- IGN map: 3432 ET – 1:25 000 Didier Richard No 11 – 1:50 000

Access: South of Albertville, cross the bridge at Albertin sur l'Isère and take the N525 to Notre-Dame-des-Millières. At the exit from the village, immediately after a small bridge, abandon the route nationale and take a private road on the left which rises in successive bends for 17 km. Go to the end of the road by the Chalet de l'Ebaudie and leave vehicles there (alt. 1,600 m).

Ascent: The summit of La Grande Lanche lies on the extreme left of the crest which dominates the Chalet de l'Ebaudie, starting point for this climb. Ignore the path straight ahead and turn right up a broad grassy slope in the direction of the crest. Shortly afterwards, on flat ground, aim boldly to the right and head for a long steep ridge leading to the crest. Get on to this and ascend the grassy and stony slope. One arrives at the crest at a sort of small col. Beyond and below that is visible the small Lac de Queige, to which one may descend easily if tempted to extend the walk. From the small col, follow the crest to the left to reach the highest point at its end in 10 minutes. To the right and in front, a secondary crest leads to a knoll topped by a cross. Alternatively from the small col, if you wish to add spice to the ascent, it is possible to follow the crest to the right to climb the adjacent summit. From this point, a second small lake, the Lac Rond, is visible below.

Descent: Descend by the same route.

Route notes

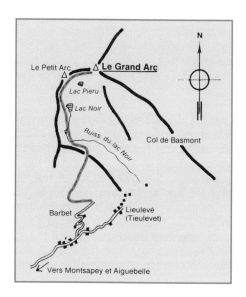

85 Le Grand Arc

- height: 2,482 m
- starting point: Montsapey (73), 32 km south of Albertville
- route: from the south
- grade: I
- climbing time: 3 hours
- views: magnificent
- type of ground: grass, stones
- IGN map: 3432 ET – 1:25 000 Didier Richard No 11 – 1:50 000

Access: From Albertville take the N525 to Aiton, the N6 to Aiguebelle and the D72 to the village of Montsapey, situated at the end of an ascent of almost 10 km. Continue beyond here and turn left into a small road signposted to Barbet. Go to its end (broken stones, then tarred) where vehicles may be left at a car park (alt. 1,630 m).

Ascent: At the end of the car park, take a path which rises northwards up a gentle slope and in less than 30 minutes reach the bottom of a grassy ridge. Cross to the other side of the ridge and descend about 20 metres towards a big valley (tricky section on a small, inclined slab). Ascend westwards on good tracks and arrive high up in the valley. Follow the stream from the Lac Noir, traverse a flat area northwards and, in the same direction, climb a rise which brings you to the edge of the Lac Noir. Follow the path to the left and reach the crest. Le Grand Arc, visible from afar, marks the end of the crest. Follow the ridge northwards (striking view to the left of the Combe de Savoie with the River Isère) and deviate briefly to contour around the easy summit of the Petit Arc. Descend to a gap (slightly tricky section) from where Lac Pieru is visible below on the right. Beyond the gap, the crest rears up sharply as a forbidding steep rise. Cross this fairly exposed section carefully. Above here the crest levels out and the summit is reached easily.

Descent: Descend by the same route.

Route notes

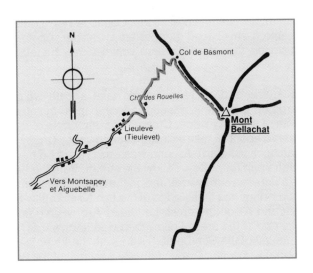

86   Mont Bellachat

- height: 2,483 m
- starting point: Montsapey (73), 32 km south of Albertville
- route: from the west
- grade: I
- climbing time: 3 hours 30 minutes
- views: magnificent
- type of ground: grass
- IGN map: 3432 ET – 1:25 000 Didier Richard No 11 – 1:50 000

Access: From Albertville, take the N525 to Aiton, the N6 to Aiguebelle and the D72 to the village of Montsapey, situated at the end of an ascent of almost 10 km. Carry on to the end of the road, in the vicinity of Tieulever where vehicles can be left (alt. 1,260 m). It is possible to continue on a metalled road as far as the Chalet des Rouelles at the top of the small valley and visible from Tieulever but make sure beforehand about parking facilities (which saves about 10 minutes).

Ascent: At Tieulever, take the track straight ahead to the Chalet des Rouelles (alt. 1,320 m). Pass the front of the chalet and traverse westwards as far as a ravine hollowed out by the torrent which descends from the Col de Basmont to the north-east, between La Grand Arc on the left and Mont Bellachat on the right. Ascend to the right up a grassy slope practically devoid of tracks, walk alongside the ravine briefly, then higher up, on approaching a patch of undergrowth, look for a well marked path which rises steeply and directly to the Col de Basmont. At the col, turn right and follow the grassy crest south-eastwards. A little further on, contour to the left, then climb a very steep rise (hard going). Continue along the broad and easier crest as far as the foot of the summit block, then go round it on the right in order to reach the peak, topped by a signal tower.

Descent: Descend by the same route.

Route notes

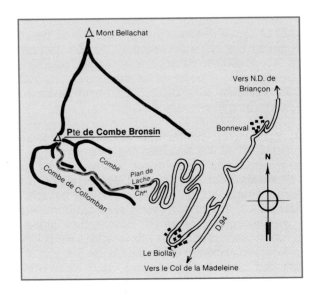

87   Pointe de Combe Bronsin

- **height:** 2,499 m
- **starting point:** Bonneval (73), 24 km south of Albertville
- **route:** from the south-east
- **grade:** I
- **climbing time:** 3 hours
- **views:** very beautiful
- **type of ground:** grass, stones
- **IGN map:** 3432 ET – 1:25 000 Didier Richard No 11 – 1:50 000

Access: From Albertville, follow the N90 in the direction of Moûtiers as far as Notre-Dame-de-Briancon, then take the D94 on the right which leads to the Col de la Madeleine. After Bonneval (6 km from Notre-Dame-de-Briancon), take the little road on the right signposted to Biollay and Lacha. A little higher up, at a bend, ignore a newly constructed road on the right. Continue to follow the road above Biollay to its end, i.e. the Plan de Lacha (alt. 1,900 m).

Ascent: From the Chalet de Lacha, dominated to the north-west by the Pointe de Combe Bronsin, head westwards up a gentle slope which continues as a long crest separating the Colomban valley on the left from that coming down from the Pointe de Combe Bronsin on the right. Ascend this crest, which narrows, and reach the Col du Loup (alt. 2,100 m) which gives access to the Combe de Colomban. Do not climb the steep shoulder beyond the col; it would be dangerous to attempt it. Without losing height, traverse across the slope of the Combe de Colomban to the base of the Pointe de Combe Bronsin on tracks which run alongside a small rocky barrier on your right. Go as far as a sort of bottleneck just after the rocky barrier and ascend the short but steep slope. Up above, aim to the right (northwards) to reach the centre of the upper slope which meets the summit crest. Ascend facing the slope and towards the top turn slightly left in order to reach the crest at its most accessible point. Turn right to reach the nearby summit.

Descent: Descend by the same route.

Route notes

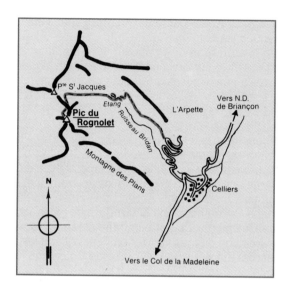

88   Pic du Rognolet

- height: 2,656 m
- starting point: Celliers (73), 35 km south of Albertville
- route: from the east
- grade: III
- climbing time: 4 hours 30 minutes
- views: very beautiful
- type of ground: grass, stones, rocks. Often large snow-fields before the final section.

- equipment necessary: rope, ice axe
- IGN map: 3433 ET – 1:25 000 Didier Richard No 11 – 1:50 000
- Hut 2000 (private)
  hut warden   Tel: 79 59 10 60

Access: Between Albertville and Moûtiers, at Notre-Dame-de-Briancon, take the D94 in the direction of the Col de la Madeleine and reach the village of Celliers (alt. 1,361 m). About 500 metres above Celliers, ignore the col road and take the one on the right which leads to L'Arpette. Higher up, cross the stream over a narrow bridge. Having crossed the bridge as well as the bend which follows, stop at the sixth hairpin (not counting the easy bends). Space for parking (on the left) is restricted (alt. 1,700 m, 3.5 km from Celliers).

Ascent: At the bend, move to the left on a more or less obvious path which heads towards an enormous valley, bordered on both right and left by long crests, with the Bridan stream flowing down its centre. Not long after starting (10 min), and before much height has been gained, abandon this line, despite the fact that it seems to be the obvious one, and climb briefly up the grassy slope on the right. Then rejoin the general upward line of the valley while searching for signs of a rather weather-worn path. Whatever happens, ascend the righthand side of the valley, with or without path. Via a succession of terraces, reach a small lake (alt. 2,030 m), nestling in a hollow and only visible at the last moment. Carry on up above the lake, aiming slightly to the left and, via another series of terraces, reach a boulder field often covered with snow, especially at the beginning of the season. Ascend the now steeper slope, heading slightly left all the time towards the jagged rocky barrier which encloses the valley. Near the base of this wall, aim boldly to the left (southwards) and ascend a sort of ridge parallel to the rocky barrier and made up of large unstable blocks. To the left of this ridge there is nearly always a steep snowfield flanked at its top by a characteristic rocky tower. The ridge narrows on the right towards the wall and then a chimney comes into sight (on the right) which you need to climb, so as to reach a gap which splits the rocky barrier (tricky section, good holds). Now emerge on to the opposite slope. Immediately start traversing left (southwards) up the terraces, taking care not to get too high. In front is the Pic du Rognolet, just to the right of a rocky tower with a big and very obvious natural reddish patch. At the end of the traverse, at the level of a small couloir on the left, turn right and traverse a boulder field which is very often filled with snow, so as to reach the first of two steep ridges of big unstable blocks, which descends directly from the summit. This section is very tricky and if you want to rope up, keep it very short to avoid dislodging rocks with the rope. Thus reach the narrow and exposed summit.

Descent: It is imperative that descent should be made the same way.

Route notes

Route notes

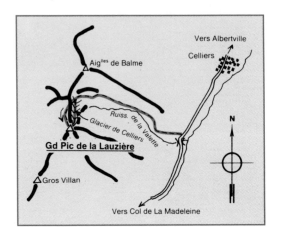

89   Grand Pic de la Lauzière

- height: 2,829 m
- starting point: Celliers (73), 35 km to the south of Albertville
- route: from the east
- grade: III
- climbing time: 4 hours
- views: very beautiful
- type of ground: grass, stones, rocks, ice
- equipment necessary: rope, ice axe, crampons
- IGN map: 3433 ET – 1:25 000 Didier Richard No 11 – 1:50 000
- Hut 2000 (private)
  hut warden   Tel: 79 59 10 60

Access: Between Albertville and Moûtiers, at Notre-Dame-de-Briancon, take the D94 in the direction of the Col de la Madelaine and reach the village of Celliers (alt. 1,361 m). The range of La Lauzière, in relation to the climber's line of ascent, is on the right. After passing through Celliers, stop at the bottom of the second big valley, near the bridge which crosses the La Valette stream (about 4 km above Celliers). Leave vehicles beside the broad road (alt. 1,600 m).

Ascent: Enter the Combe de la Valette and ascend a more or less well marked path on the true left bank of the stream (right when climbing). Pass a stable and ascend a large grassy slope, aiming for a big hillock high up in the middle of the valley in front of the rocky barrier which encloses it. When level with this knoll, the small Glacier de Celliers is visible higher up on the left. Start off left of the knoll and ascend a boulder field in the direction of a big rocky face. Follow the foot of this face to the left to reach the glacier. From this point on, the terrain changes abruptly and becomes alpine. Roping up is recommended here. Climb the right hand side of the glacier close to the long rocky crest which terminates at the Grand Pic de la Lauzière. A deep crevasse is often open halfway up the glacier. Cross it carefully or go round it. Leave the glacier on the right at the spot where the rocky crest is lowest. Then climb to the left up the short ridge made up of unstable blocks which leads to the narrow summit. The far side is exposed.

Descent: Descend by the same route or, well beyond the summit, go left to rejoin the top of the glacier and lower down retrace your line of ascent (remain roped up while on the glacier).

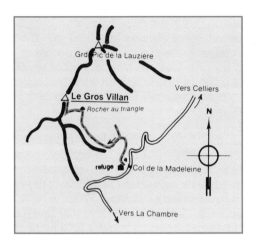

90 Le Gros Villan

- height: 2,746 m
- starting point: Celliers (73), 35 km south of Albertville; Saint-Francois-Longchamps (73), 23 km north of Saint-Jean-de-Maurienne
- route: from the east
- grade: II
- climbing time: 3 hours 30 minutes
- views: very beautiful
- type of ground: grass, stones, rocks
- equipment necessary: rope
- IGN map: 3433 ET – 1:25 000 Didier Richard No 11 – 1:50 000
- Hut 2000 (private)
  hut warden   Tel: 79 59 10 60

Access: Two possibilities:
1) *Tarentaise side.* Between Albertville and Moûtiers, at Notre-Dame-de-Briancon, take the D94 via Celliers to the Col de la Madeleine.
2) *Maurienne side.* Between Aiguebelle and Saint-Jean-de-Maurienne, at La Chambre, take the D213 and follow it to the Col de la Madeleine. Leave vehicles in the car park on the col (alt. 1,993 m).

Ascent: Coming from the direction of Celliers, take a good path on the right behind the café and contour to the right past a big grassy hillock which dominates the col. A little further on (about 15 min), leave the path, which rises north-westwards towards the range of La Lauzière, and follow tracks to the left behind the hillock. Ascend a sort of small hemmed-in valley and near its head turn right (westwards). Climb a grassy slope, locating the scattered blocks with red paint marks. Keep going westwards all the time facing the line of the slope. Higher up, the slope eases towards the end of the grassy area, in the vicinity of a big boulder field strewn with big blocks. Tackle the boulder field on the right, taking a sighting on an isolated rock below the summit ridge of Le Gros Villan on which is painted a big red triangle. Ascend above this rock to the triangle, aiming slightly left, to reach the knife-edge ridge via a steep stony slope. Follow this to the right (exposed) and go round or climb the easy rocks. The section of ridge to be crossed is not long. To emerge on to the summit, cross a tricky section slightly below the ridge on the eastern side (good holds).

Descent: Descend by the same route.

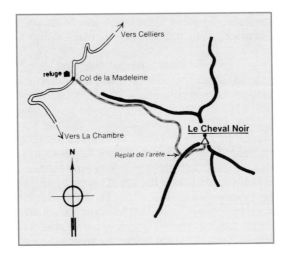

91 Le Cheval Noir

- height: 2,832 m
- starting point: Celliers (73), 35 km south of Albertville; Saint-Francois-Longchamps (73), 23 km north of Saint-Jean-de-Maurienne
- route: from the west
- grade: I
- climbing time: 3 hours
- views: magnificent
- type of ground: grass, stones
- IGN map: 3433 ET – 1:25 000 Didier Richard No 11 – 1:50 000
- Hut 2000 (private)
  hut warden   Tel: 79 59 10 60

Access: Two possibilities:
1) *Tarentaise side.* Between Albertville and Moûtiers, at Notre-Dame-de-Briancon, take the D94 to the Col de la Madeleine via Celliers.
2) *Maurienne side.* Between Aiguebelle and Saint-Jean-de-Maurienne, at La Chambre, take the D213 and follow it as far as the Col de la Madeleine. Leave vehicles at the car park on the col (alt. 1,993 m).

Ascent: If arriving at the Col de la Madeleine from the direction of Celliers, Le Cheval Noir lies at the end of the long ridge to the left (south-east) beyond the initial grassy slopes. Take a track in this direction and follow it briefly as far as a pylon. Ascend to the right up the grassy slope as if to join the ridge but, at the foot of a big and very upright knoll, aim to the right and descend slightly in the direction of a large valley, so as to contour around this hillock. Pass behind it and reach a relatively flat area at the foot of a big boulder field which comes down from the summit of Le Cheval Noir. From this point you need to pinpoint landmarks for the rest of the route, as tracks are non-existent. Ahead is the long ragged crest which starts from Le Cheval Noir and descends southwards. Follow the line of the crest from the summit towards the south (i.e. from left to right) until you see a big flat area in front of a very marked break. One should emerge on to the crest at this flat area. Head upwards by making first a rising traverse to the right. Soon after, a rough area composed of enormous blocks appears. Contour right around this. At the level of the flat area on the crest, climb facing the very steep slope. Progress is hard going on unstable scree. Reach the more welcoming crest at the point indicated and ascend it to the left on a good path. A little higher up as you approach the summit, the slope becomes extremely steep. Reach the peak by two big rising traverses (tough going), first to the right and then to the left.

Descent: It is imperative that descent by made by the same route.

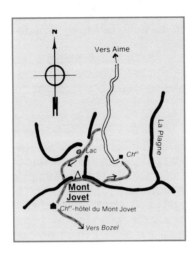

92 Mont Jovet

- height: 2,554 m
- starting point: Longefoy (73), 21 km north-east of Moûtiers
- route: from the north
- grade: I
- climbing time: 1 hour 30 minutes
- views: magnificent
- type of ground: grass
- IGN map: 3532 ET – 1:25 000 Didier Richard No 11 – 1:50 000
- Mont Jovet Hut (CAF)
  hut warden   Tel: 79 08 11 20

Access: From Moûtiers take the N90 to Aime. On the other side of the town, take the La Plagne road on the right and leave it 2 km further on to turn right on to the D88 in the direction of Longefoy. After passing through Longefoy, immediately take a small road on the left which rises in steep zig-zags. Pass the hamlets of Montalbert and Montgesin. Higher up the road climbs through pastures, then enters a small valley in which it follows the western side. Stop at the point practically opposite the top of the La Plagne ski lift, the pylons of which can be seen on the slope opposite (alt. 2,050 m).

Ascent: Continue briefly on the road, then ascend to the right a path way-marked in yellow. Very soon reach a small crest and follow it to the left for a short while. Traverse right under the spurs of Mont Jovet and reach a small lake. Continue westwards, following the base of the mountain as far as a small col. Then aiming to the left, climb the western slope which leads to the summit provided with its view indicator.

Descent: Follow the crest eastwards along the summit ridge, losing height. At the level of a small col, descend to the left and reach a large basin, then aiming left again reach the chalet which marks the end of the road on which you started lower down.

Route notes

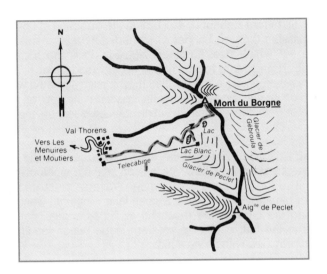

93 Mont du Borgne

- height: 3,152 m
- starting point: Saint-Martin-de-Belleville (73), 19 km south of Moûtiers
- route: from the south-west
- grade: II
- climbing time: 2 hours 30 minutes
- views: magnificent
- type of ground: stones, rocks
- IGN map: 3534 ET – 1:25000 Didier Richard No 11 – 1:50000

Access: From Moûtiers on the N51A, Saint-Martin-de-Belleville and Les Menuires to Val Thorens, the end of the road (alt. 2,300 m). Leave vehicles south of the station, near the Glacier de Péclet télécabine.

Ascent: Ascend a ski piste left of the Glacier de Péclet télécabine cables, as far as a building site road. Turn left on to this road (signposted to Lac Blanc) and follow it as far as a sign pointing to the lake. Leave the road there and ascend the slope north-eastwards to a second lake, lying in the middle of a cirque. Continue north-eastwards (no track) and ascend the steep scree slope (hard going) which descends from the crest between the Mont du Borgne on the left and the Glacier de Péclet on the right. Get on to the crest just to the right of the Mont du Borgne, near a very slight rift in the crest. Follow the practically flat crest to the base of the short terminal ridge. Climb the steep rocks of the ridge to the very exposed summit.

Descent: Descend by the same route.

Route notes

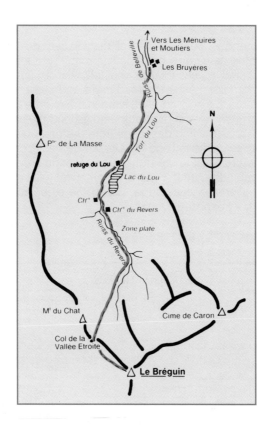

94 Le Breguin (or Brequin)

- height: 3,135 m
- starting point: Saint-Martin-de-Belleville (73), 19 km south of Moûtiers
- route: from the north
- grade: II
- climbing time: 4 hours 30 minutes
- views: magnificent
- type of ground: grass, stones, often snowed up at the start of the season
- IGN map: 3534 ET – 1:25000 Didier Richard No 11 – 1:50000
- Lou Hut (community property)
  hut warden   Tel: 79 00 61 43 (guides bureau)

Access: From Moûtiers on the N515A to the station of Les Menuires (Belleville valley). Take the Val Thorens road and immediately after passing the starting point of the La Masse télécabine, take a little road on the right to the hamlet of Les Bruyères where vehicles can be left (alt. 1,766 m).

Ascent: Cross the bridge over the River Belleville and ascend southwards on a good path up the small Lou valley down which flows a raging torrent. Reach the Lou Hut (alt. 2,055 m) which overlooks the prettily situated Lac du Lou (alt 2,030 m). Walk alongside the lake on the right and continue uphill (southwards), following the righthand side of the Revers stream. Reach an isolated chalet not far from the lake and at this level cross the stream to the left, either on planks or by fording it, so as to continue the ascent on the opposite bank. Pass the Chalet du Revers and climb a gentle slope which reaches a vast flat area at the junction of several streams. Cross the Ruisseau de Revers again to reach the top of this area. Avoid going into the big valley straight ahead. Aim to the right and ascend a fairly steep stony slope near and to the right of a torrent gushing from the upper level. Up above, the slope eases again and to the south the long crest which runs to Le Breguin (extreme left) is visible: The ridge drops deeply to the right, forming the broad Col de la Vallée Etroite. Head for the col, avoiding the valley on the left which seems to lead more directly to the summit. From the col, follow the ridge briefly to the left, then when this becomes impracticable, continue below on the right. Rejoin the top of the ridge after a big rocky tower and proceed easily to the summit, topped by a signal.

Descent: Descend by the same route.

Route notes

Route notes

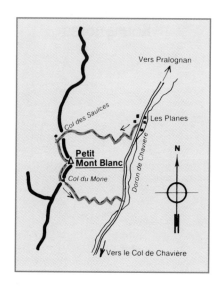

95 Petit Mont-Blanc

- height: 2,678 m
- starting point: Pralognan (73), 28 km south-east of Moûtiers
- route: from the east
- grade: I
- climbing time: 3 hours
- views: very beautiful
- type of ground: woodland, grass, stones
- IGN map: 3534 ET – 1:25 000 Didier Richard No 11 – 1:50 000
- Chalet Gîte Le Petit Mont-Blanc Hut (private)
  hut warden   Tel: 79 08 72 73

Access: At Moûtiers (N90 Albertville-Bourg-Saint-Maurice), take the N515 as far as Pralognan-la-Vanoise. At the beginning of Pralognan, by a signpost to the town, turn right and head south-wards to reach the head of the Pralognan basin. Turn right again and ascend a small road which enters a pretty little valley, dominated by the Glaciers de la Vanoise to the east. Continue as far as the chalets at Les Planes (alt. 1,585 m) and leave vehicles by the side of the road, near a signpost on the right to the Col des Saulces-Petit Mont-Blanc (about 3 km from Pralognan).

Ascent: By the signpost mentioned above, take a path which rises in zig-zags up a steep, wooded slope (hard going). Higher up at about 2,000 metres, the angle slackens and the well marked path winds pleasantly around numerous holes hollowed out by erosion. On the right a deep and curiously eroded ravine is visible. Le Petit Mont-Blanc lies at the highest point of the crest which dominates the slope to the left. Continue westwards and reach a cirque of meadows in front of the Col des Saulces (alt. 2,457 m) which is visible at its head. On entering this cirque, aim boldly to the left and tackle the vast bare brow of Le Petit Mont-Blanc. The peak is easily reached.

Descent: Descend by the same route. It is equally possible, and is moreover recommended, to descend by continuing beyond the summit as far as the Col du Mone, lying just below. From the col, turn left and, on a good path, rejoin the road a little above your starting point. Take care between the col and the road to avoid the tracks which go off to both left and right by staying with the line of the slope.

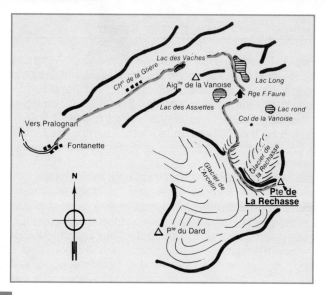

96 Pointe de la Réchasse

- height: 3,209 m
- starting point: Pralognan (73), 28 km south-east of Moûtiers
- route: from the north
- grade: II
- climbing time: 1st day: 3 hours; 2nd day: 3 hours
- views: magnificent
- type of ground: stones, rocks, ice
- equipment necessary: rope, ice axe, crampons
- IGN map: 3534 OT and 3633 ET – 1:25 000
  Didier Richard No 11 – 1:50 000
- Faure (De La Vanoise) Hut (CAF)
  hut warden   Tel: 79 08 25 23

Access: At Moûtiers (N90 Albertville-Bourg-Saint-Maurice), take the N515 and follow it as far as Pralognan-la-Vanoise. At the beginning of Pralognan, turn left and by a little road which rises eastwards reach the hamlet of Les Fonanettes. Leave vehicles in the car park on the left (alt. 1,640 m).

Ascent: First day: Straight on from the car park, take the broad path, signposted to the Félix-Faure Hut, which rises fairly steeply up through a wood. At the end of the short wooded section, enter a little valley where the slope becomes gentler. Pass the Chalets de la Glière (alt. 2,050 m) and continue towards the head of the valley. The slope steepens again until you near the Lac des Vaches (alt. 2,310 m), a sort of large shallow pond of elongated shape which you cross in the middle on a row of large flat stones. The lake is overlooked on the right by the impressive slabs of the Aiguille de la Vanoise. Higher up the path bends to the right to contour the Aiguille de la Vanoise and approaches Lac Long, dominated on the left by the imposing mass of the Pointe de la Grande Casse. Continue uphill to the right of the sharp bend to reach the Félix-Faure Hut, situated on the big flat area which is the Col de la Vanoise (alt. 2,510 m).
Second day: From the hut, cross the grassy plateau south-westwards, then turn to the left (southwards) on good tracks in the direction of the rocky barrier which makes up the outer base of La Réchasse. After a stoney area, ascend the barrier by a system of ledges. Then cross straight across it as soon as its angle declines. Climb a slab, often rendered tricky by streaming melt water, then climb the rocks mixed with snow and emerge on to the Glacier de la Réchasse. Traverse this to the right by following a relatively flat area, then turn left and climb the fairly steep glacier slope. Tackle the ridge on the right at its most accessible point and follow it eastwards. You can easily reach the summit, where a statue of the Virgin has been erected.

Descent: It is imperative that descent be made by the same route. It is dangerous to wander about. (Danger!)

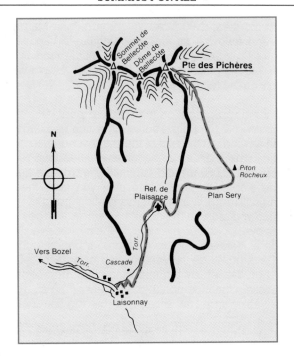

97 Pointe des Pichères

- height: 3,304 m
- starting point: Champagny-en-Vanoise (73), 19 km east of Moûtiers
- route: from the south
- grade: II
- climbing time: 1st day: 1 hour 30 minutes; 2nd day: 4 hours 30 minutes
- views: magnificent

- type of ground: grass, stones, ice or snow
- equipment necessary: ice axe, crampons
- IGN map: 3534 OT and 3633 ET – 1:25 000
  Didier Richard No 11 – 1:50 000
- Plaisance Hut (CAF)
  hut warden   Tel: 79 55 05 79

Access: From Moûtiers on the N515 in the direction of Pralognan to Bozel. At the exit from Bozel, take the D91 on the left sign-posted to Champagny and carry on beyond this village to Laisonnay-d'en-Haut at the end of the road (alt. 1,600 m).

Ascent: First day: Take a good path by the edge of the road which leads eastwards (signposted to Plaisance Hut) and which rises in zig-zags up a very steep slope to the right of a magnificent waterfall. Emerge into a small valley and ascend it northwards as far as the Plaisance Hut (alt. 2,160 m), property of the Parc National de la Vanoise.
Second day: Behind the hut, take a good path and cross the torrent to the right over a bridge. Ascend eastwards up a fairly steep slope to reach a first level, then continue above as far as a sort of small plateau which stretches northwards. Go right across this and at the end climb a short slope on the right which gives access to the Plan Séry, a vast flat area. Head eastwards with the Plan Séry on your left, then turn northwards in the direction of a characteristic rocky tower situated at the start of the long, broad crest which leads to the Pointe des Pichères. Pass below and to the left of this rocky point and ascend the mixed scree and snow crest towards the north-west. Parallel to the crest, tackle the Glacier des Pichères and ascend the steep slope which leads to the summit section. Climb some big snowy humps to reach the summit.

Descent: Descend by the same route.

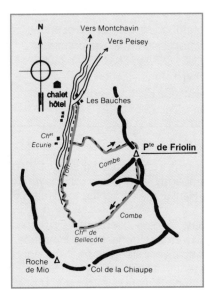

98 Pointe de Friolin

- height: 2,643 m
- starting point: Bellentre (73), 19 km north-east of Moûtiers
- route: from the west
- grade: I
- climbing time: 3 hours
- views: magnificent
- type of ground: woodland, grass, stones, rocks
- IGN map: 3532 ET – 1:25000 Didier Richard No 11 – 1:50000
- hut: Chalet Hotel Val Sante (private)
  hut warden   Tel: 79 07 84 52

Access: From Moûtiers via the N90 in the direction of Bourg-Saint-Maurice to Bellentre. Take the road on the right in the village signposted to Montchavin, which rises in broad zig-zags. Pass just left of the village of Montchavin, beside the V.V.F. (Village Vacances Famille = State-subsidized holiday village), and continue up the road as far as the Chalets des Bauches (alt. 1,771 m). Cross the bridge to the left and leave vehicles just after the chalets on a large platform.

Ascent: Beside the bridge, take the path which ascends left of the stream in a southerly direction. Follow it for about 15 minutes as far as a broad level area facing a mountain chalet and a small stable on the other side of the stream, by the edge of the track which leads to the Chalet de Bellecôte. Leave the path here and turn left (no tracks to start with) towards a wood. Traces of an old path are soon evident. They rise first of all facing the slope, then traverse horizontally left before turning right to follow the line of the slope again. Make sure you do not go astray on this section where the tracks are least apparent. On leaving the wood, one arrives at level ground. Traverse this to the right in the direction of a large valley which goes up on the left up a boulder field. Above it, tackle a steep, grassy slope mixed with rocks and keep on as far as the crest, to arrive at the point where it becomes rocky. Follow the crest to the right and climb the big blocks which buttress the first rocky point. Continue up towards the second point which is topped by a signal tower marking the summit.

Descent: From the summit, traverse a big hollow and reach the grassy crest to the south. Below the crest, get into a big valley and descend it as far as the Chalet de Bellecôte. Take the path on the right and rejoin the chalets at Les Bauches.

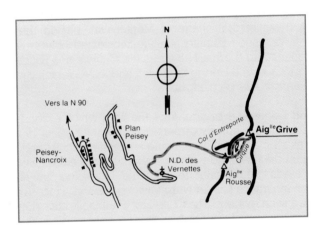

99 Aiguille Grive

- height: 2,732 m
- starting point: Peisey-Nancroix (73), 31 km north-east of Moûtiers
- route: from the west
- grade: I
- climbing time: 3 hours
- views: magnificent
- type of ground: woodland, grass, stones
- IGN map: 3532 ET – 1:25 000 Didier Richard No 11 – 1:50 000

Access: Between Moûtiers and Bourg-Saint-Maurice, on the N90 near Bellentre, take the D87 to Peisey-Nancroix. Continue for about 1 km and turn left in the direction of Plan-Peisey. By the station entrance, take the little road on the right which leads to Notre-Dame des Vernettes. Reach the chapel where vehicles can be left nearby (alt. 1,810 m).

Ascent: At Notre-Dame des Vernettes, take the path on the left signposted to the Col d'Entreporte which rises up a not very steep slope through a wood. Approach a ski piste and ascend it as far as the mountain pastures. Continue on up, aiming to the right in a rising traverse and, via a steep slope, reach the Col d'Entreporte (alt. 2,407 m) which gives access to a sort of cirque dominated at its head by the Aiguille Grive. From the col, climb the ridge on the left, on the cirque side, as far as a gap, then make a traverse below the summit (still on the cirque side). Now face the slope and ascend directly to the peak (view indicator).

Descent: From the summit, descend the scree slope in the cirque as far as the level of the Col d'Entreporte, then return by the route of ascent.

Route notes

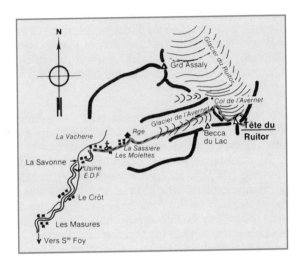

100 | Tête du Ruitor

- height: 3,486 m
- starting point: Sainte-Foy-Tarentaise (73), 12 km south-east of Bourg-Saint-Maurice
- route: from the south-west
- grade: III
- climbing time: 1st day: 1 hour; 2nd day 5 hours
- views: magnificent
- type of ground: stones, snow, ice
- equipment necessary: rope, ice axe, crampons
- IGN map: 3532 ET – 1:25 000 Didier Richard No 11 – 1:50 000
- Sassière Hut (CAF)
  hut warden   Tel: 79 06 90 12; or 79 06 92 12

Important recommendations for this route: if misty, do not go beyond the Col d'Avernet. Do not descend on to the Ruitor glacier: only skirt its edge.

Access: From Bourg-Saint-Maurice on the N90 to Séez and the N202 to Sainte-Foy-Tarentaise. At the exit from the village, in the direction of Val-d'Isère, take the small road on the left signposted to Crôt and Miroir. Follow this beyond Crôt and above the Savonne electricity works (E.D.F.) as far as a group of chalets (alt. 1,850 m). It is possible to continue higher on a rougher road, as far as a small valley and the chalets of La Vacherie (alt. 1,950 m). This saves 30 minutes.

Ascent: *First day:* On a well marked path, ascend the small valley eastwards to reach the chalets of Les Mollettes, situated at the beginning of the Plan de la Sassière. Continue towards the end of the plateau as far as the Chalets de la Sassière (alt. 2,033 m) which are for the most part in ruins. One of them has been turned into a mountain hut by the CAF. Plan to spend the night here.
Second day: From the Chalets des Sassières, head towards the slopes to the east and go straight up for a short distance. Then, turning to the left, make a traverse and get on to the Glacier de l'Avernet (prudent to rope up here). Climb its true left bank (i.e. the righthand side) up the long glaciated slope made up of successive terraces, going round at least several crevasses. The final slope which gives access to the Col d'Avernet is really steep and crampons and ice axe are required. Emerge on to the col and then the vast Ruitor glacier plateau. Aim immediately to the right and, following the edge of the plateau, make an enormous circular sweep south, north and east to reach the other bank of the glacier and the foot of the Ruitor, a big rocky hillock. Walk alongside this and on the right reach the north-east ridge and climb it to the summit (statue of the Virgin).

Descent: It is imperative that descent should be made by the same route.

contents

3. Bornes

4. Aravis

5. Bauges

6. Beaufortain

7. Vanoise-Tarentaise